SURFING

SURFING
The Ultimate Guide

Douglas Booth

GREENWOOD GUIDES TO EXTREME SPORTS
Holly Thorpe and Douglas Booth, Series Editors

GREENWOOD

AN IMPRINT OF ABC-CLIO, LLC
Santa Barbara, California • Denver, Colorado • Oxford, England

Library of Congress Cataloging-in-Publication Data

Booth, Douglas.
   Surfing : the ultimate guide / Douglas Booth.
      p. cm. — (Greenwood guides to extreme sports)
   Includes bibliographical references and index.
      ISBN 978-0-313-38042-6 (alk. paper) — ISBN 978-0-313-38043-3 (ebook)
   1. Surfing.   I. Title.
   GV840.S8B66   2011
   797.3'2—dc22   2010051946

ISBN: 978-0-313-38042-6
EISBN: 978-0-313-38043-3

15   14   13   12   11   1   2   3   4   5

This book is also available on the World Wide Web as an eBook.
Visit www.abc-clio.com for details.

Greenwood
An Imprint of ABC-CLIO, LLC

ABC-CLIO, LLC
130 Cremona Drive, P.O. Box 1911
Santa Barbara, California 93116-1911

This book is printed on acid-free paper ∞

Manufactured in the United States of America

To Gaye, who looks over me in the South Pacific.

contents

series foreword

of interest to students and enthusiasts alike, extreme sports are changing and redefining the nature of physical activity around the world. While
baseball, soccer, and other conventional sports typically involve teams,
coaches, and an extensive set of rules, extreme sports more often place the
individual in competition against nature and themselves. Extreme sports
have fewer rules, and coaches are less prominent. These activities are
often considered more dangerous than conventional sports, and that element of risk adds to their appeal. They are at the cutting edge of sports and
are evolving in exciting ways.

Extreme sports are fascinating in their own right; they also offer a window on popular culture and contemporary social issues. Extreme sports
appeal most to the young, who have the energy and daring to partake, and
who find in them alternative cultures with their own values and vocabu-
lary. At the same time, some extreme sports, such as surfing, have long
histories and are important to traditional cultures around the world. The
extreme versions of these sports sometimes employ enhanced technology
or take place under excessively challenging conditions. Thus they build
on tradition yet depart from it. Extreme sports are increasingly significant
to the media, and corporations recognize the marketing value of sponsor-
ing them. In this way extreme sports become linked with products, their
star athletes become celebrities, and their fans are exposed to a range of
media messages. Local governments might try to regulate skateboarding
and other extreme activities, sometimes out of fear for safety and sometimes out of moral concerns. Yet other communities provide funding for
skateboard parks, indoor rock climbing facilities, and such venues for extreme sports enthusiasts. Either way extreme sports are an indelible part of
contemporary civil discourse.

Designed for students and general readers, this series of reference books
maps the world of extreme sports. Each volume looks at a particular sport

and includes information about the sport's history, equipment and techniques, and important players. Volumes are written by professors or other authorities and are informative, entertaining, and engaging. Students using these books learn about sports that interest them and discover more about cultures, history, social issues, and trends. In doing so, they become better prepared to engage in critical assessments of extreme sports in particular and of society in general.

Holly Thorpe and Douglas Booth, Series Editors

preface

I tackled surf-riding and now that I have tackled it, more than ever do I hold it to be a royal sport. . . . Ah, that delicious moment when I felt that breaker grip and fling me. On I dashed, a hundred and fifty feet, and subsided with the breaker on the sand. From that moment I was lost.

Jack London (1911, 69 and 73)

shortly after the publication of *The Encyclopedia of Extreme Sports* in 2007, my co-editor on that project, Holly Thorpe (University of Waikato), received an invitation to edit a series of books, each dealing with an individual extreme sport. As well as extending a generous offer to join her in co-editing the series, Holly invited me to write the edition on extreme surfing. I readily accepted.

I enjoy extreme sports. I appreciate, perhaps even envy, the extraordinary, gravity-defying athleticism and coordination of the most skilled exponents. Equally appealing is the philosophy of extreme sports, which focuses on pleasure through creative and free movement—speeding, sliding, gliding, falling, rotating, what Roger Caillois (1958/2001) called *ilinx* (vertigo)—in natural and built environments. Although extreme sports are framed by social and cultural interpretations and meanings, they also seem to exude a higher level of raw biological (genetic, hormonal, physiological) pleasure, which serves as a welcome counter to overhyped, overglossed, overcommercialized established sports. Unbounded by space and time, and focused on individuals, extreme sports largely escape the extraneous interests of myopic and insular fans, salacious spectators, zealous officials, authoritarian coaches, corporate hangers-on, conservative ideologues, moral crusaders, and sanctimonious journalists who variously follow, associate with, and report and comment upon established elite team sports and mega sporting events. How long extreme sports can remain free from these agents and forces remains to be seen; the signs in surfing and snowboarding are sadly ominous. In the interim. . . .

The term extreme typically connotes risk and exposure to injury. Exposure to injury is a universal trait of all physical activity, regardless of how innocuous (e.g., showering, descending stairs, crossing roads). Before undertaking a physical activity, whether as part of day-to-day life, work, or leisure, most people will consider, either consciously or subconsciously, the level of risk. Continuation with the activity thus involves calculations and the adoption of strategies to reduce the probability of injury (e.g., holding on to a rail to prevent slipping in the shower; wearing a life vest to guard against drowning in big surf). However, no universal standard of objective risk exists in established sports or extreme sports; participants define their own level of risk, and an activity that one individual considers risk free, another may define as high risk. Moreover, individuals constantly reappraise their calculations of risk; what appears high risk at one moment might seem perfectly safe the next—and vice versa. Joe Tomlinson illustrates the complexity of risk calculations in the case of BASE jumping when he lists "the most important skill any BASE jumper can possess" as "the ability to differentiate between a jump that can be made, and one that can but shouldn't" (Tomlinson 2004, 15).

Notwithstanding the willingness of participants to accept some risk, minimization of the risk threshold has been a hallmark of the codification of sports and ongoing changes to rules in different codes. Among the better known early examples of rules intended to reduce the risk of injury are the mandating of "fair size" gloves in boxing in 1867 and the Rugby Football Union's 1871 prohibition against "hacking" (kicking an opponent to the ground). More recent examples of risk reduction include safety equipment (e.g., mouthguards in Australian football, helmets in cricket, full-face shields in ice hockey, frangible [breakable] fences in equestrian events) and rule changes (e.g., the ban against "spearing" [using the top of the helmet when tackling an opponent] in American football, the prohibition against checking from behind in ice hockey).

The mania for risk in extreme sports—captured by the "If it can't kill you, it ain't extreme" special tow-in surfing contest (http://www.towsurfer. com)—suggests that devotees accept higher levels of danger than participants in established sports. Statistical evidence seems to provide confirmation. In climbing and air sports the estimated death rate is about 800 per 100 million person-days, compared with 70 for water sports, 30 for horse riding, 16 for rugby, and 5 for boxing. Yet, on closer inspection, high risk per se does not stand out as a characteristic of extreme sports. Many activities labeled "extreme" are actually very safe. Sports journalist Rick Arnett might call bungee jumping "suicide on-a-string" (Arnett 2006) but statistics show it is no more dangerous than riding a roller coaster.

Such comparisons suggest an alternative approach to understanding extreme: thrill as a state of physiological arousal. As responses to perceptions of danger, senses of vertigo, and acute stress, physical thrills trigger specific physiological actions that are collectively and popularly known as an "adrenaline rush." On perceiving a stimulus, the brain relays signals through the central nervous system. This process initiates the release of the hormones epinephrine and norepinephrine into the blood, which in turn causes stimulatory reactions throughout the body, including increases in heart rate and breathing, and the redirecting of blood into potentially active muscles. An accumulation of epinephrine and norepinephrine may "overload" the system and precipitate spontaneous or intuitive behaviors popularly described as "fight or flight." Some physiologists believe that in other cases these stimulatory reactions may enable individuals to maintain control in chaotic situations and avoid fear-induced paralysis. Describing a version of the control response, big-wave legend Laird Hamilton (2002) advises surfers to "listen to your instincts, if they are saying don't go then there is a reason." Some researchers also hypothesize that these physiological mechanisms may produce an addiction to thrill-seeking behavior; the body also releases dopamine in response to arousal, and this hormone is involved with the sensation of pleasure and accomplishment. Anecdotal evidence supports this hypothesis. Riding "powerful, beautiful and scary" waves, says Hamilton (2002), bestows "a calmness over you that you can't really explain." Hamilton's peer Dave Kalama agrees: the experience of riding extreme waves and "being that close to death makes you feel alive" (*Extreme Surfing* 2000, ch. 6).

Anthropologists and sociologists, on the other hand, analyze risk within the context of physically based, hierarchical cultures that celebrate and glorify risk. In these cultures, risks constitute challenges, and meeting these challenges earn members—predominantly young men—rewards (e.g., peer recognition and prestige). Far from highlighting their strategies to minimize risk, members of these cultures embellish their calculations. A common bedfellow here is the media, which happily regales readers with stories of young men risking all to prove their mettle.

Regardless of the analytical framework, no evidence indicates that disciples of extreme sports have completely abandoned concerns for safety.
On the contrary, most participants in extreme sports reject the label of
risk takers; they are no less conscious of safety than participants in established sports. In his study of high-risk competitors, including skydivers, racing car drivers, and aerobatic pilots, Bruce Ogilvie (1974)
concluded that they are success oriented and rarely reckless risk takers.
Their risk taking, he said, is cool and calculated. Similarly, Joe Tomlinson dismisses notions of extreme sports disciples as "fanatics seeking a
buzz" without regard for consequences. He argues that they all "perform
within their limits" (Tomlinson 2004, 6). Typical accounts of extreme
sports emphasize the importance of safety, equipment, and support. Big-
wave rider Ross Clarke-Jones likened the preparations to surf Dangerous
Banks (northwest Tasmania) in 2007 to a military operation; a helicopter provided a visual overview of the surfers and the drivers of the personal watercraft (PWC) who towed the riders into the waves. The PWC
were equipped with radios that enabled the drivers to contact each other
and the helicopter pilot. The surfers and PWC drivers each carried a flare
(*Storm Surfers* 2007, ch. 7). Of course, as the statistics cited imply, the
nature of the environment means that the consequences of failure tend to
be more severe in extreme sports than established sports.

I am an active surfer but I make no claim to practicing extreme versions. There are few penalties for making mistakes when surfing small
waves. Over four decades, I have received the occasional stitch from colliding with my board. Once, a wall of white water caught me unaware at
South Curl Curl (Sydney, Australia) and dragged me along an elevated
shore platform; on another occasion, a raging current swept me over half
a mile along the coast at Raglan (New Zealand). But these events did not
threaten life or limb and so in this sense they fall outside the definition of
extreme, a realm where the forces of nature allow little room for errors
in judgment or technique (Brymer, Downey, and Gray 2009, 194). Although I have never entered the extreme realm, I believe my surfing experiences and research into the sociology, history, and culture of the sport
(e.g., Booth 2001a) equip me to write this book. What follows, then, is a
guide to extreme surfing framed by personal experiences and honed by
scholarly analysis.

Surfing: The Ultimate Guide captures the essentials of big-wave surfing, which John Long (1999, 4) eloquently describes as "among the greatest adventure sports in terms of its rich history, classic milestones, colorful

characters, controversies, all-time performances, startling innovations, hilarious and tragic events, and the vein of true grit that runs through all the top performers." The book comprises seven chapters. In chapter 1, I explain the concept of extreme as it applies to the cultural and physical environments of surfing. I examine the history of big-wave riding in chapter 2 in three eras and places: ancient Hawai'i, the 1950s and '60s on the North Shore of O'ahu (Hawai'i), and the period since the early 1990s, which is associated with the global development of tow-in surfing. In chapter 3 I delve into two scientific aspects of extreme surfing: the science of waves—the weather and ocean conditions that predispose and precipitate giant surf—and the biological sensations, or affects, of riding waves that make it a pleasurable experience. Following this scientific excursion, I describe the oceanography and geography of selected sites at which the largest surfable waves break (in chapter 4) and the attributes and feats of legendary extreme surfers (in chapter 5). Extreme surfing is a highly skilled pursuit, and in chapter 6 I examine some of the key technical aspects, notably around equipment, training, and rescues, before concluding in chapter 7 with a look into the future.

A number of people provided invaluable sources, advice, and help in compiling this book: Holly Thorpe, Michelle Alexander, Gaye Booth, Geoff Booth, Jose Borrero, George Butler, Robin Canniford, Graham Carse, Jim Cotter, Mike Cronin, Mark Falcous, Kevin Fisher, Brendan Hokowhitu, Annemarie Jutel, Geoff Kohe, John Loy, Kimberly O'Sullivan Steward, Greg Page, Murray Phillips, Steve Pope, Richard Pringle, Bob Rinehart, Teresa Smith, Mark Stevenson, and Kristi Ward. I extend my appreciation and gratitude to them.

Douglas Booth (University of Otago), Dunedin, 2010

chronology

A.D. 600–700
Surfing established in Hawai'ian Islands.

1778
On his third expedition to the Pacific aboard the HMS *Discovery* and *Resolution,* Captain James Cook makes the first recorded European visit to Hawai'i. Hawai'ians kill Cook at Kealakekua Bay on the Kona Coast of the Big Island, Hawai'i. Lieutenant James King on board the *Discovery* continues writing Cook's journals and provides the first known description of Hawai'ians surfing, which he calls a pleasant amusement.

1820s
British missionary William Ellis notices Hawai'ian surfers "standing erect in the midst of foam." Surfing declines as Western diseases ravage the Hawai'ian population and Calvinist missionaries discourage the activity they deem unproductive.

1866
American author Mark Twain spends several months in the Hawai'ian Islands and tries his hand at surfing. After an unsuccessful attempt, he concludes that "none but natives ever master the art of surf-bathing."

1874
February 12: David Kalākaua elected king of Hawai'i. He encourages a cultural revival of old Hawai'ian sports and pastimes, including surfing.

1883
November 8: George Freeth born in Honolulu. Freeth will be among the first of his generation to ride across the wave; he will be instrumental in the revival of surfing at Waikiki in the early 20th century. Jack London will refer to Freeth as "a sea god...calm and superb."

1885

July 20: The *Santa Cruz Daily* provides the first known account of surfing in California when it reports Jonah Kūhiō Kalaniana'ole, David Kawānanakoa and Edward Keli'iahonui—nephews of Queen Kapi'olani, queen to Hawai'i's King Kalākaua—surfing at the mouth of the San Lorenzo River, Monterey Bay. At the time the trio were enrolled at St. Matthew's Military School in San Mateo.

1890

August 24: Duke Paoa Kahanamoku is born. By age 15 Kahanamoku, tutored by George Freeth, will be regarded as the best surfer at Waikiki; ultimately, Kahanamoku will receive the title of father of modern surfing.

1891

January 20: King Kalākaua dies, and surfing declines in popularity over the next decade.

1903–8

Surfing is revived as the Hawai'ian pineapple, sugar, and tourist industries experience a boom and Hawai'ians and visitors rediscover surfing. The tourist industry promotes Waikiki as a romantic and exotic holiday destination. Duke Kahanamoku and other surfing devotees regularly gather at a *hau* tree on Waikiki beach and experiment with boards and riding styles.

1907

May: American novelist Jack London visits Hawai'i. London meets the surfing enthusiast and later founder of the Outrigger Canoe Club Alexander Hume Ford, also a recent arrival in the Islands, and George Freeth. Ford encourages London to try surfing, and the latter's account of his experience and a detailed explanation of the sport will be published a few months later in *Woman's Home Companion*.

October: George Freeth surfs at Venice Beach, California. Shortly after, Freeth becomes the state's first professional lifeguard.

1908

December 12: George Freeth rescues the crew of a capsized Japanese fishing vessel during a violent storm.

1911

Duke Kahanamoku and his brothers co-found Hui Nalu (Club of the Waves) primarily for Hawai'ian athletes who are excluded from Alexander Hume Ford's Outrigger Canoe Club on the grounds of their social class.

Jack London republishes his 1907 essay on surfing in his travelogue *The Cruise of the Snark.*

1914–15
Summer: Duke Kahanamoku tours Australia and New Zealand, where he demonstrates surfing to large audiences.

1917
Summer: Duke Kahanamoku rides a wave at Waikiki from Outside Castles to the shoreline at Queens, a distance of 1¾ miles.

Circa 1918
First known report of a modern surf riding contest in Hawai'i with contestants judged on form. The report appears in *Hawaiian Surfriders, 1935,* written by Tom Blake, the highly influential mid-20th-century surfboard designer.

Late 1937
John Kelly and Wally Froiseth lead groups of Honolulu surfers to Makaha and the North Shore.

1943
December 22: Honolulu surfer Dickie Cross drowns at Waimea Bay when he and Woody Brown are caught inside by 30-foot waves.

1953
November 27: Newspapers across the United States publish a photograph of George Downing, Buzzy Trent, and Wally Froiseth riding a large wave at Makaha. The photograph inspires a number of Californian surfers to head to the Islands.

1954
September 26: Bob Simmons drowns while surfing at Windansea, San Diego, after his board hits him in the head. Surfing historian Matt Warshaw later calls Simmons "the primary architect of the modern surfboard...who almost single-handedly brought into play the now fundamental principles of nose-lift, foil, and finely sculptured rails."

1956
November–December: A team of American lifeguards, which includes surfers Greg Noll, Tom Zahn, Mike Bright, and Bobby Moore, demonstrate Malibu surfboards in Australia. Invited by Surf Life Saving Australia for a special Queen's International Carnival coinciding with the olympic games in Melbourne, the lifeguards surf before enthralled crowds at Torquay and Avalon.

1957

November 7: Greg Noll leads Bob Bermel, Del Cannon, Harry Church, Bing Copeland, Pat Curren, Mickey Muñoz, and Mike Stange into 15- to 18-foot surf at Waimea.

1960

Fred Hemmings paddles out at Pipeline but wipes out on his one wave.

1961

Mid-December: Phil Edwards successfully rides Pipeline on consecutive days. His waves featured in Bruce Brown's *Surfing Hollow Days* (1962).

1964

November: Greg Noll rides a 25-foot wall at Outside Pipeline; Bud Browne films the ride for his film *Locked In* (1964).

1967

November 20: Eddie Aikau launches his career at Waimea Bay in the biggest swell of the decade to that point. The *Honolulu Advertiser* later labels Aikau "Mr. Waimea."

1969

December 4: At the peak of the swell of '69, Greg Noll paddles-in to a 30-foot-plus wave at Makaha. It will remain the largest wave ridden until the early 1990s.

1974

October 3: Felipe Pomar claims to have ridden a tsunami at La Isla, Peru.

November 28: The semifinals and final of the Smirnoff Pro are held in 25-foot-plus waves at Waimea Bay; Reno Abellira narrowly defeats Jeff Hakman.

1975

Winter: Jeff Clark begins surfing Maverick's on a regular basis.

1976

July 24: Big-wave rider Jose Angel, whom Greg Noll called the "gutsiest surfer there ever was," dies while free diving at Shark Ridge, Maui.

1977

November 28: Eddie Aikau wins the Duke [Kahanamoku] Classic in solid 8- to 12-foot surf at Sunset Beach with a classic deep tube ride. He concludes his acceptance speech with the words, "we have to love each other and take care of each other 'cause you never know when your time is going to come."

1978
March 17: Eddie Aikau leaves the stricken *Hōkūle'a* on a 10-foot board in rough seas to paddle 12 miles to Lāna'i Island for help. Later in the day a rescue boat picks up the 15 remaining crew members from the *Hōkūle'a* but finds no trace of Aikau.

1984
December: The first contest held to commemorate Eddie Aikau is staged at Sunset Beach. The contest, won by Denton Miyamura, subsequently shifts to Waimea Bay and becomes a big-wave event conducted only when the surf breaks over 20 feet.

1985
January 18: A rising swell produces some of the biggest waves ever to hit Waimea Bay. Ken Bradshaw dominates the morning session until his board is broken and he struggles ashore. Four surfers—Mark Foo, James Jones, Alec "Ace Cool" Cooke, and J. P. Patterson—stay in the water. A rogue wave of unprecedented magnitude closes out the bay and catches them inside. When they resurface Foo is the only one with a board still attached to the leg rope; a rescue helicopter lifts the three boardless riders from the water. Foo waves away the helicopter before attempting an impossible take-off on a 30-foot concave wall. This time when he resurfaces Foo welcomes the rescue helicopter pilot's offer of a ride to the beach. Legendary big-wave rider Peter Cole, who watches these events unfold from his car, thinks Foo shows a "lack of judgement" throughout. Later Foo will cleverly exploit his experience, described in great detail in the surfing press, to project himself as "Waimea Man."

1987
February 21: Clyde Aikau wins the big-wave contest named after his brother Eddie ahead of Mark Foo (second) and Ken Bradshaw (third). The cover of *Surfer* magazine's contest edition featured Foo wearing an Eddie contest singlet printed with the number 1 under the headline "winning moves."

December: Herbie Fletcher tows Martin Potter and Tom Carroll in to waves at Second Reef Pipeline using a personal watercraft.

1990

January 21: Keone Downing wins the Eddie Aikau memorial contest.

1991

Winter: Buzzy Kerbox and Laird Hamilton experiment with tow-in surfing at Phantoms using a 40-horsepower engine attached to a Zodiac.

1992

Winter: Darrick Doerner joins Buzzy Kerbox and Laird Hamilton towing-in on the outer reefs of the North Shore; they now use a 60-horsepower engine.

1992–93

Winter: Buzzy Kerbox and Laird Hamilton experiment with tow-in techniques at Pe'ahi (Jaws).

1993–94

Winter: The "Strapped Crew"—Mark Angulo, Pete Cabrinha, Darrick Doerner, Laird Hamilton, Dave Kalama, Brett Lickle, Rush Randle, and Mike Waltze—become the vanguard of tow-in surfing.

1994

December 19: Jay Moriarty endures a spectacular wipeout at Maverick's that receives wide publicity in the mainstream media.

December 23: Mark Foo drowns at Maverick's in his first session at the break.

1995

December 23: Donnie Solomon drowns at Waimea Bay.

1997

February 13: Todd Chesser drowns at Outside Alligators.

1998

January 28: Huge surf batters the North Shore on the day known as "biggest Wednesday" in surfing lore. The surf forces the cancellation of the Eddie Aikau contest, and many extreme riders head to the outer reefs where Dan Moore tows Ken Bradshaw on to an 80-foot face at Outside Log Cabins. At Jaws the "Strapped Crew" ride 30-foot-plus waves.

January 30: Hawai'i's "biggest Wednesday" swell reaches California, where it closes out most breaks. Surfer Ken "Skindog" Collins describes the bigger sets at Maverick's as "tubing death wishes."

1999

January 1: Noah Johnson wins the Eddie Aikau memorial contest.

March 22: Sarah Gerhardt successfully surfs Maverick's, helping to debunk the myth of extreme surfing as a purely male pursuit.

2000

August 17: Legendary waterman Laird Hamilton rides what many consider the most ferocious and deadliest wave ever ridden at Teahupo'o.

2001

January 12: Ross Clarke-Jones wins the Eddie Aikau memorial contest. Reflecting on the significance of the contest and his win, Clarke-Jones says, "A single day contest, four waves...[and]...38 seconds on a surfboard consumed 15 years of my life."

June 15: Maverick's regular Jay Moriarty drowns while free-diving in the Maldives.

2002

January 1: Garrett McNamara and Rodrigo Resenda win the first tow-in competition, the 2001–2002 Tow-In World Cup event at Jaws.

January 7: Kelly Slater wins the Eddie Aikau memorial contest.

2004

December 15: Bruce Irons wins the Eddie Aikau memorial contest.

December 26: A magnitude 9.0 earthquake at the interface of the India and Burma tectonic plates, 250 kilometers (150 miles) south-southeast of Banda Aceh, Northern Sumatra, generates the Indian Ocean tsunami that kills an estimated 150,000 people and leaves millions more homeless.

2005

December 2: Malik Joyeux, renowned extreme surfer from Tahiti, drowns at Pipeline.

2009

May 13: Former women's world champion Layne Beachley joins the Bra Boys at the intensely local Sydney break, Ours. Beachley's session includes a tow-in to a heavy barrel that will earn her a nomination for the Ride of the Year in the 2010 XXL Global Big Wave Awards.

August 11: Maya Gabeira rides a 20-foot-plus wave at Dungeons that some claim is the biggest wave ever ridden by a woman.

December 8: Greg Long wins the Eddie Aikau memorial contest.

December 27: The "Dream Crew"—Grant Baker, Alfy Carter, Nathan Fletcher, Mark Healey, Greg Long, Rusty Long, Pete Mel, Ramon Navarro (winner of the Monster Drop Award at the 2009 Eddie Aikau Memorial), and Kelly Slater—enjoy glassy paddle-in conditions at Cortes Bank.

2010

July 9: Professional surfer Joel Parkinson wipes out at his home break (Snapper Rocks, Queensland) and collides with his surfboard. The fin on the board slices through tendon and muscle in Parkinson's heal and the injury forces him to miss the next six events on the world professional tour. Parkinson returns to competitive surfing in mid November, scoring a perfect 10 in his first heat in the first event of the prestigious Triple Crown of Surfing—a combination of three events on the North Shore of Oʻahu, the Hawaiʻian Pro (Haleiwa), World Cup of Surfing (Sunset Beach), and Pipeline Masters (Pipeline)—which he wins for the third consecutive year.

November 2: Three-time world surfing champion Andy Irons found dead in a hotel room in Dallas with the cause unknown (at the time of writing). As well as "the most fearless surfer at some of the world's heaviest breaks, often riding deep inside the tube at … Pipeline and Teahupo'o," Irons had a "legendary temper" and "a reputation for wild behavior off the water." Significantly, he was, in the word's of surfing historian Matt Warshaw, "the only worthy rival" to Kelly Slater (Melekian 2010. *See also* "Surfer Andy Irons" 2010).

November 6: Thirty-eight year old Kelly Slater wins his tenth World Title which he immediately dedicates to Andy Irons. "If it wasn't for Andy," Slater declared, "I wouldn't be here right now" (Walker 2010, slide 11).

1. explanations

[S]uddenly, out there where a big smoker lifts skyward, rising like a sea-god from out of the welter of spume and churning white, on the giddy, toppling, overhanging and downfalling, precarious crest appears the dark head of a man. Swiftly he rises through the rushing white. His black shoulders, his chest, his loins, his limbs—all abruptly projected on one's vision. Where but the moment before was only the wide desolation and invincible roar, is now a man, erect, full statured,...not buried and crushed and buffeted by those mighty monsters, but standing above them all, calm and superb, poised on the giddy summit, his feet buried in the churning foam, the salt smoke rising to his knees, and all the rest of him in the free air and flashing sunlight, and he is flying through the air, flying forward, flying fast as the surge on which he stands. He is a Mercury—a brown Mercury. His heels are winged, and in them is the swiftness of the sea.

Jack London (1911, 67–68)

in the popular imagination, surfing is a classic extreme sport: every boardrider battles collapsing mountains of water, violent turbulence, frenzied sharks, razor-sharp coral heads, and boulder-strewn reefs. A torrent of stories, films, and photos reinforce these popular images. A picture of Jay Moriarty free-falling down the face of a 20-foot wave at Maverick's (Northern California) in December 1994 appeared in the *New York Times;* NBC's *Nightly News* showed footage of the wipe-out. Laird Hamilton's ride across a 20-foot wall at Teahupo'o (Tahiti) in August 2000 received front-page coverage in the *Los Angeles Times* and won the Action Sports Feat of 2000 at the annual ESPN Action Sports Awards. The international media reported the shark attack on

13-year-old surfer Bethany Hamilton at Haʻena (Kauaʻi) in October 2003. Hamilton, who lost her left arm just below the shoulder, subsequently appeared on the *Oprah Winfrey Show* and gave interviews to *Glamour* magazine and CBS's *Entertainment Tonight.* In *Billabong Odyssey* (2003), the narrator of the aptly subtitled DVD *The Search for the World's Biggest Wave,* attributes the "mystique" of surfing to devotees who appear "comfortable in an environment" that "absolutely terrifies... the average person."

Contrary to these images, surfing is a fairly safe activity with a rate of injury no higher than that for fishing. The average surfer incurs four injuries (deep cuts, sprains, fractures, and so forth) every 1,000 days of riding (Renneker, Star, and Booth 1993, 274). Most injuries happen in waves under four feet high as a result of surfers colliding with their own surfboards or the ocean bed. Shark attacks, drownings, and deaths are rare. This rarity, paradoxically, draws attention from a hysterical media which further fuels the popular imagination of a wildly dangerous pastime. In the mid-1990s the media widely reported a spate of accidents that saw the deaths of three big-wave riders. Mark Foo drowned on December 23, 1994, after wiping out on a 15-foot wave at Maverick's (Warshaw 2000) (see chapter 4). Years earlier he had prophetically warned that those seeking "the ultimate thrill" would "pay the ultimate price" (Warshaw 1987, 63). Donnie Solomon died at Waimea Bay, the shrine of big-wave riding on Oʻahu (Hawaiʻi) (see chapter 4), one year to the day after Foo's death (Warshaw 2000, 187 and 191). Todd Chesser drowned at Outside Alligators, a reef west of Waimea Bay, on February 13, 1997 (Marcus 2008, 66–67).

Reflecting on the statistics, surfer journalist and author of *The Encyclopedia of Surfing* Matt Warshaw (1995a, 102) observes that surfing fatalities are "rare" and that the sport does not bear comparison with truly dangerous pastimes such as "bull fighting, autoracing, or mountain climbing." Thus, the "extreme" label appears something of a misnomer when applied to surfing. However, I embrace the term in two senses. First, the irreverent culture of surfing and its associated lifestyle conjures notions of extreme as in "outside the normal." Second, many of the best waves explode in shallow water overlying coral heads and boulder beds, and surfers who ride these breaks (sites of surfing waves) risk severe physical injury. In this chapter I explain the cultural dimensions of surfing as well as the various physical risks.

culture

Although "rediscovered" at the turn of the 20th century, the ancient Polynesian art of surfing did not become popular until the mid-1950s. Technology posed an initial obstacle to the development of surfing in the early 20th century. Made of solid wood, early surfboards were heavy and impossible for all but the most highly skilled to ride. In the 1950s California surfers produced shorter, lighter, and highly maneuverable boards made of balsa wood. These Malibu boards, named after the beach where they came to prominence, made surfing more accessible, and the activity burgeoned in California. Anthropologist John Irwin (1973) estimates that the surfboard-riding population of Southern California grew from 5,000 in 1956 to 100,000 in 1962. Assisting the diffusion of surfing were Hollywood surf films (e.g., *Gidget, Muscle Beach*), "pure" surf films made by devotees (e.g., *Slippery When Wet, The Big Surf, Surf Trek to Hawaii*), and surfing magazines (e.g., *Surfer, Surfing, Surfing World*) (Moore 2010).

Many young surfers who adopted an irreverent, hedonistic culture drew critical comments from their elders, members of a generation whose life perspectives were forged in economic depression and world war. Social commentators in the 1950s and early 1960s condemned surfing as an indolent, wasteful, selfish, and institutionally unanchored pastime. Surfers' appearance, the "trademark" of which was long, bleached hair; their irreverent argot, humor, and rituals; and their nomadic lifestyle rendered them socially irresponsible in these people's minds. Bruce Brown, producer and director of the classic surfing adventure film *The Endless Summer* (1966), well remembers parents and nonsurfing peers chiding him for "wasting time" and urging him to "do something useful" (Kampion 1997, 21). Greg Noll, who became a legend of surfing (see chapter 5), recalls one exchange with a school principal when he was a boy:

> "What do you guys do down there at the Manhattan Beach Surf Club? What are your goals, what do you want to become?" I told him that I wanted to surf, I wanted to make surfboards, I wanted to go to Hawaii, I wanted to see the world and have a good time. From the principal's point of view, that qualified me as most likely to end up a beach bum and never amount to shit. (Noll and Gabbard 1989, 31)

In Australia, where surfing culture developed quickly behind California, surfers also attracted bad publicity and press. One observer referred to surfers as "useless": they "cruise from beach to beach looking for the best surf" and "pay no rates or fees of any kind, frequently not even parking fees" (Titchen 1966). Others denounced "long-haired" surfers who "took over footpaths for their boards, public toilets for changing rooms, made unofficial headquarters of public facilities," and passed loud "rude" and "foul" remarks at girls (*Manly Daily* [Sydney, Australia] October 15 1965; *Daily Telegraph* [Sydney] February 13 1964).

In the early 1960s some surfers attempted to negotiate a more accept-able cultural style and expression by defining themselves as sportsmen and women. To this purpose they established new regional and national associations, and they organized competitions to take surfing into the mainstream sporting world. Initially they appeared to have succeeded. Lewis "Hoppy" Swarts, the inaugural president of the United States Surf-ing Association, noted with pride that competitions had "helped develop a new image with the public—the public has come to respect our surfers in the same way as they respect other athletes" (*Surfer* May 1968, 27). A Sydney newspaper echoed Swarts's sentiment, praising surfers' new-found "maturity" since they had formed an official body (*Manly Daily* May 15 1964). Big business and vested political interests flocked to surf-ing. Sponsors of the first official world surfing championships, at Manly Beach (Sydney) in May 1964, included Manly Council, Ampol (Petro-leum), and TAA (Trans Australian Airlines). They were blunt about their motives: "Manly will get a lot of publicity from international television coverage of the event," said mayor Bill Nicholas (*Manly Daily* April 16 1964). The championships were a phenomenal success—an estimated crowd of 65,000 watched Australian Bernard "Midget" Farrelly win the crown. A senior Ampol representative described surfing as "the fastest growing sport in Australia" and pledged his company's ongoing support (*Manly Daily* May 19 1964).

But organized competition required formal rules, and codification was no simple matter with surfing styles reflecting regional variations, par-ticularly between California and Australia: Australians wanted to slash and conquer waves; Californians sought waves for artistic expression. Debate over style fueled dissension over judging methods and scoring and led to accusations of corruption, cronyism, and nepotism. The result was a significant decline in competitive surfing in the late 1960s, a wan-ing reinforced by the counterculture. An amalgam of alternate, typically utopian, lifestyles and political activism, the counterculture emphasized self-realization and encouraged individuals to pursue their dreams through a distinctive "new left" politics that embraced anti-authoritarian gestures, iconoclastic habits (in music, dress, language, and lifestyle), and a general critique of everyday life.

Soul-surfing—riding waves for "the good of one's soul"—articulated this new politics and critique, and it conjoined surfing with the counter-culture. Soul-surfers scorned the constraints of organized surfing. Henry "Kimo" Hollinger, a big-wave rider and anticontest crusader, captures well the general animosity toward competitive surfing. He was surfing Waimea Bay in 1975 as the Smirnoff contest (see chapter 4) began:

> The kids started paddling out with numbers on their bodies. Numbers! It was incongruous to the point of being blasphemous. I wondered about myself. I had been a contestant and a judge in a few of those contests when it all seemed innocent and fun. But it never is. The system is like an octopus with long legs and suckers that envelop you and suck you down. The free and easy surfer, with his ability to communicate so personally and intensely with his God, is conned into playing the plastic numbers game with the squares, losing his freedom, his identity, and his vitality, becoming a virtual prostitute. And what is even worse, the surfers fall for it. I felt sick. (Hollinger 1975, 40)

Under the influence of the counterculture, soul-surfers applied increasingly esoteric interpretations to surfing: waves became dreams, playgrounds, podia, and even asylums, and the search for perfect waves became an endless pursuit.

Surfing signified self-expression, escape, and freedom. Australian surfer Robert Conneeley (1978, 18) described surfing as "the ultimate liberating factor on the planet"; fellow traveler Ted Spencer (1974, 10) claimed that he "dance[d] for Krishna" when he surfed; and former world champion turned soul-surfer Robert "Nat" Young (1970, 7) believed that by the simple virtue of riding waves, surfers were "supporting the revolution." The tabloid media, however, found no merit in a youth-led social revolution. It accused surfers of not washing and of being undisciplined, indulgent, and decadent. Sydney's *Sun-Herald,* for example, called them "jobless junkies" (April 19, 1971). Many surfers did consume drugs, and some were members of drug networks comprising investors, organizers, traffickers, and dealers (Jarratt 1997, 70–73 and 78–84; Kampion 1997, 127–32). Nonetheless, the tabloid media's depictions of surfers too often descended into gross caricatures.

> **stoked**   The essence of counterculture soul-surfing was "stoke." To ride a wave was "to stoke the fires of the heart and soul" and hence to be stoked (Grissim 1982, back cover).

Ultimately, the counterculture was unsustainable. Yet, the counterculture did contribute to the development of professional surfing: its work-is-play philosophy encouraged one group of surfers to establish a professional circuit in the belief that it would offer them an economic avenue to eternal hedonism (Tomson 2008).

Today, surfing is a widely organized and accepted sport. Surfers compete for honors, as amateurs and professionals, at local, regional, national, and world levels. Yet, most surfers subscribe to the irreverent culture of the early founders, and many continue to question the place of competition and professional surfing in particular: polished images portrayed by professional surfers to win broad public appeal simply do not resonate with members of the antiestablishment surf culture. As soon as people in the 1970s "tried to turn 'surfing the artform' into 'surfing the sport' surf culture suffered," complains Kit (*TransWorld Surf* August 8, 1999), a correspondent who echoes the sentiments of thousands and illustrates something of an extreme cultural perspective.

Unlike traditional sports, which are organized around set times and clearly demarcated spaces, surfing depends on unpredictable and fickle Mother Nature to generate the waves upon which surfers play. Traditionally (in the early 20th century) surfers simply waited at their favorite beach for the arrival of waves. After the Second World War, a surge in private vehicle ownership and cheaper airfares gave surfers more mobility, and freedom, to search for waves (e.g., McTavish 2009). Traveling in search of waves became known as a *surfari,* in surfing lingo. In the mid-1960s Bruce Brown portrayed the ultimate surfari in *The Endless Summer* (1966), which followed California duo Robert August and Mike Hynson's worldwide search for perfect waves.

The surfari is not just a search for waves; it also symbolizes a cultural release from mundane life. *Tracks* correspondent "One-of-eight" (October 2005, 51) captures this aspect of the surfari in his description of a four-day "boys weekend... to escape the [winter] chill, our wives and the kids." The weekend provided great waves but produced even greater stories. "I've never laughed so hard in all my life," "One-of-eight" wrote. Reflecting on the companionship, he added, "it was fantastic to sit there with a group of blokes...digging up forgotten misadventures from 20 years ago, and I guess that's the point—we all felt 20 years younger."

Some surfers extended the surfari into a "feral" existence, traveling to remote surf breaks and camping for extended periods. The feral surfer, says surfer journalist Michael Fordham (2008, 96), "sacrifices all worldly desires in pursuit of his obsession. He has seen the surf dream and is determined to live it." In the 1950s, ferals camped on the North Shore of O'ahu (see chapter 2): "Many of them lived like Bedouins on the beach, surfing all day and partying like Beatniks late into the night" (Coleman 2004, 46). In the 1970s surfing films such as Albie Falzon's *Morning of the Earth* (1972) and articles in surfing magazines glamorized feralism, "further tempting thousands of adventurous young surfers to take flight" (Fordham 2008, 96). Later, entrepreneurially motivated ferals began organizing and operating surf camps and charter boats from their bases. Tony Hinde, for example, founded Atoll Adventures in the Maldives in 1990 after basically surfing the islands alone for the previous fifteen years (Fordham 2008, 96).

The feral surfer, the "committed wave-riding survivalist who remains at a parasite infested jungle camp for months on end" (Fordham 2008, 96), still exists. California surfers Timmy Turner, Travis Potter, and Brett Schwartz recently went feral for three months on Palau Panaitan (Indonesia). "Armed with just their boards, fishing gear, rice, noodles, water, chickens, a goat, Tylenol, cigarettes and not much else, the boys had been camped on the island alone for weeks risking malaria, reef cuts, and...castaway madness." The waves by their camp made it all worthwhile, even though they had to wear wetsuits in the tropical heat to "avoid being sashimied on the reef, days away from medical help." "It's hard doing this, being away," Turner confessed in his diary, "but I love it over here. Going feral is the greatest thing" (Doherty 2008, 44th moment).

Yet, if the surfari is a defining characteristic of surfing culture, the nomadic surfer, paradoxically, exposes a dark side of surfing: localism. At the heart of localism lie issues around ownership of individual waves and surfing breaks, and individual and collective cultural identities. Not infrequently, disagreements over these issues erupt in violence. Under surfing lore (i.e., conventions, unwritten rules, rituals, codes of conduct), the rider on the inside, closest to the breaking wall, "owns" the wave. But securing the inside position at any break requires physical skill, cultural knowledge, and political acumen. South African surfer Craig Jarvis's account of paddling-in to the lineup at Jeffreys Bay—perhaps the best right break in the world—graphically illustrates these attributes:

> It's a quick and easy paddle out, and I reached the line up with my hair still dry. When I approached the takeoff zone I sat on my board, clearly on the inside of...two guys. This local guy looks at me and snaps, "What the f**k you doing?" I reply, "Gonna catch a few waves. What's the problem?" He replies tersely, "the problem is, if you want to catch a wave you have to wait in queue. And the f****n queue starts right here!" he slaps the water next to him. I look at him and he glares back. Neither of us backs down. So I lie on my board and paddle straight towards him. We both keep full, beady eye contact all the way. I paddle right up to him, turn around next to him and straddle my board again, so close our legs are almost touching. We stick our chests out like peacocks. "No problem," I reply matter-of-factly. "No problem," he replies. (Jarvis 2001, 63)

This exchange ended on friendly terms—"turns out we had a bunch of mutual friends," Jarvis (2001, 64) recalled—but some do escalate (Evers 2009, 79). One highly publicized assault occurred at Angourie Beach (New South Wales, Australia) in 2000 and left Nat Young with multiple fractures to his face that required six and a half hours of reconstructive surgery (Young 2000, 18–19).

At popular urban and tourist breaks, inexperienced surfers will often "clog up the peak, section and bowl" and frustrate experienced locals who might "have to miss the section and go around someone just sitting clueless and in the way" (Marcus 2008, 32). Or worse, they can pose safety hazards. In *The Book of Surfing* Michael Fordham relates how one day in the mid-1980s the "core crew" were in the water at Bondi Beach (Sydney) when "a big, pale, hairy-armed German" paddled out on a "battered old longboard." He clearly "didn't know what he was doing" and "was way out in front of the pack when the set started to show":

> It was a sneaker...that had formed into a menacing black line filling the horizon. He was never going to make it over the top so he should have just bailed to cut his loses. But, not knowing any better, as the first wave of the set started to feather, he continued to paddle right up into the lip. As the crew saw what was about to happen, there were curses as they gathered to dive as deep as they could. The lip started to throw and the guy, all 200 pounds of him, ten feet

of Volan-glassed log and ten inches of hatchet fin came backwards, flailing fast and deadly through the crowd. Once the set had passed, the German guy came up to the surface, laughing, looking around at the other surfers paddling in boiling water.

But the "heavy, testosterone-laden" crew did not share the pleasure:

A tiny young larrikin paddled up to the German and began screaming at him. He had a great gash on his cheek where the fin had sliced him. A moment later he was joined by another guy, and then another, and soon the smile slipped off the German's face as the sharp, short blows started to rain down on his head as the pack rounded on him like piranhas. (Fordham 2008, 228)

Some participants and commentators defend such vigilante justice on the grounds of preserving order and safety at surf breaks. Ten-time world champion surfer Kelly Slater believes it works at Pipeline (Oʻahu) (see chapter 4): the intensity of the wave there "means you're going to have people who are just as intense. That's where they live and that's their backyard and no one's going to come in and try to just have their way with the place. It's kept in order" (Olsen and Higgins 2009). However, in many instances, claims by locals that they are preserving order and safety is a thinly disguised defense of privileges—priority over waves in the water, and priority over sun, shade, or parking on the beach (Evers 2009, 81).

Some commentators, such as former *Tracks* editor Sean Doherty, conceptualize localism in terms of harmless geographically based tribes which provide surfers with their sense of identity (*Bra Boys* 2006, ch. 5). However, there are numerous examples of surfer tribes descending into brotherhoods or fratriarchies. Under the control of leaders who "claim the right not only to the best waves, but also the right to grant waves to the lesser ranks in the hierarchy" (Fordham 2008, 229), brotherhoods actively "exclude non-resident surfers through threat, intimidation and occasionally violence" (Warshaw 2004, 340). John Philbin "threw rocks, stole boards off unknown cars, waxed windows, and let air out of the tires of countless unlucky strangers" trying to surf at Palos Verdes (California) (Marcus 2008, 86). Philbin admits that he was simply doing what "the older, cool surfers, my heroes, did or told me to do, in order to gain their respect or trust or admiration and ultimately to get good waves when the swells came" (Marcus 2008, 84). Some surfing fratriarchies use initiation rites, or hazing, to control and discipline members. At Narrabeen (Sydney), for example, older surfers regularly tied younger surfers—"grommets"—to the grommet pole, locked them in the rage cage (a wire basket used by lifesavers to detain stray dogs), or simply buried them up to their necks in the sand. In one particular instance

> they tied Robbo and Skiddy's arms behind their backs and buried them up to their necks about two metres apart, facing each other with only their heads sticking out of the sand. They had to have a spitting competition. They had to hack gollies at each other's heads. Robbo lost so they got his scum dog, Bandit, that used to hang around the carpark and shimmied Robbo's face with Bandit's arse. (Abraham 1999, 53)

The sense of ownership, the sense of priority over non-locals, and expectations that everyone must obey local lore and authority adds weight to the argument put forward by sociologist and surfer Clif Evers (2009, 84) that "there is no overarching sense of safety," rather "safety for one group [means] a threat to another" (see also Evers 2010). Nowhere is Evers's cultural context of safety more evident than in the two best-known surfing brotherhoods, the Wolfpak (formerly Da Hui) and the Bra Boys, which operate on the North Shore (Oʻahu) and Maroubra (Sydney) respectively.

Da Hui, more formally Hui O He'i Nalu (Club of Wave Sliders), emerged in the 1970s along with rising political activism, the resurgence of indigenous Hawaiʻian consciousness and identity, and concerns among local surfers that visitors did not afford them due respect (Coleman 2004, 165–68; Pawle 2009). In the mid-1970s a small group of pretentious and posturing Australians wounded Hawaiʻian pride and offended Hawaiʻian dignity in a series of "chest-beating" claims about dominating North Shore surfing competitions and breaks (e.g., Bartholomew 1976). Their bragging generated considerable resentment, and early in the winter of 1976–77, two Hawaiʻians assaulted Wayne "Rabbit" Bartholomew, the brashest and most outspoken of the Australians, in the surf at Sunset Beach, pounding his head and face while holding him underwater (Bartholomew 1996, 150–51). A few days later, the legendary Hawaiʻian big-wave rider Eddie Aikau (see chapter 5) visited Bartholomew at his hotel refuge. Aikau made clear his disapproval of Bartholomew's behavior and warned him of contracts on his life. According to his biographer Stuart Holmes Coleman (2001, 190–91), Aikau believed the situation had gone too far and advised that his family was seeking a resolution. Aikau returned a few days later and directed

Bartholomew to attend an open meeting at which he would be tried for crimes against the Hawai'ian people. Speaking at the meeting, Solomon "Pops" Aikau declared the situation could be easily resolved: "You Aussies gotta learn to be humble" (Jarratt 1977a). Those at the meeting agreed Bartholomew could stay on the North Shore and surf, although there were also warnings that no one could protect him from acts of random violence (Bartholomew 1996, 155; *Bustin' Down the Door* 2008, ch. 9).

In the 1990s the Wolfpak effectively succeeded Da Hui, many members of which had ceased surfing (Messer 2009), although the latter name survives as a cult clothing line sold at surf shops in nearly two dozen states and a dozen countries (Trebay 2008). The Wolfpak gained public notoriety in 2008 when one of its most prominent members, Kala Alexander (and another, unidentified person), appeared in a YouTube clip savagely beating another surfer (see Olsen and Higgins 2009). "We were just sticking up for our beliefs and our neighborhood and our families," Alexander insisted. "When people ask me about my aloha, I tell them the aloha spirit was burned right out of Hawai'ian people," he added (Trebay 2008). However, a string of public comments by prominent Wolfpak members and associates suggest that the demand for respect is very much "one way" (Evers 2009, 85). "When I go out to surf, don't bother me, don't bother my kids, don't bother the other kids around here. Just stay out of the way," warns Eddie Rothman, a co-founder of Da Hui (Warshaw 2004, 279). After former world champion Sunny Garcia chased Brazilian Neco Padaratz out of the water during the Pipeline Masters contest for an alleged indiscretion, the surfer insisted, "it's my backyard, I can do what I like" (Pawle 2009). According to Eddie Rothman's son Makua, "this is our spot, this is our waves, we live here year round.... When we're going, even if we're in front of you or in back of you, we have right of way. It's just respect" (Melekian 2008).

The surf is a focal point for many young male residents of Maroubra, a working-class suburb 10 miles south of Sydney harbor, and in the shadow of Australia's infamous Long Bay prison. Kelly Slater considers Maroubra the "most localized surf community" he has encountered (*Bra Boys* 2006, ch. 1). Maroubra has a long history of surfer gangs dating back to the 1950s, and records show these gangs fighting rivals from other suburbs in every decade. In the early 1990s, gang rivalries again escalated and Maroubra's surfing youth coalesced into a group known as the Bra (short for Maroubra) Boys under the leadership of three brothers: Sunny, Koby, and Jai Abberton.

A dysfunctional family life saw the Abbertons find kinship in each other and their fellow surfers, to whom they turned for understanding, support, and respect. Surfing, reflects Sunny, "has saved so many kids around here and led into a lifestyle in the ocean instead of a lifestyle in crime." All three brothers have surfed in professional contests, and Koby is a reputable big-wave rider. Koby likens the Bra Boys to "Mums and Dads to so many kids in Maroubra. You go down there and you know you are going to be taken care of. Any kid can come down here and in a strange way Maroubra will take care of you" (*Bra Boys* 2006, ch. 9).

Most explanations of the contemporary surge in extreme sports focus on individual temperaments and the apparent psychological need for some individuals to find meaning by risking their lives (see chapter 3). However, the references to fratriarchal relationships above alert us to sociological factors. Big-wave riders constitute a warrior caste in surfing; riding giant waves bestows the greatest prestige. Indeed, irrespective of the era and performance in organized competitions, surfers have always reserved the most prestige for those who show excess courage in big waves. Prestige is a resource in all sporting cultures, and it is a resource for which there is intense competition. While the primary function of a culture is to build social consensus, this does not eliminate competition for prestige. On the contrary, competitors are the building blocks of many cultural groups (Barnes 1995, 147). Displays of physical prowess and courage in big waves still carry the most prestige in surfing (see also chapter 5). When Laird Hamilton arrived at Tavarua (Fiji) during a contest on the professional tour in 2005, he allegedly reduced the professional surfers to "starstruck grommets, and the grommets to blubbering jellyfish" (Doherty 2005, 26). While the professional tour surfers competed for championship points in six-foot waves at Restaurants, hardcore big-wave riders competed for cultural capital by risking their bodies and reputations in 20-foot waves at Cloudbreak.

As well as navigating cultural extremes, extreme surfers immerse themselves in hostile natural environments. The simple act of surfing entails physical risks at each of the three stages of a surfing session: getting into the water, negotiating and riding waves, and returning to land.

risks

Surfers are highly literate. They

spend their lives reading waves, surveiling weather charts and satellite photos and doing the math. They read the way swells appear on the horizon and shift toward the shore, the way they hit the point, the reef, the sandbar, the jetty. Surfers read waves to find the best take-off spot, the best place to paddle (or tow) in, the best place to hit the first turn. Surfers read the sections of a wave—the bumps, flat spots, hollow spots, power spots. They read where to turn, where to cut back, where to pull into the tube, where to get out. (Marcus 2008, 18)

How well surfers read the surf conditions during a session will in large part determine their experience and pleasure. But there are always hazards and risks.

In some cases, just getting to the water can be a serious mission. On surfari along a remote stretch of New South Wales, Clif Evers (2006, 229–30) remembers "the tone of the crashing waves echoing down the valley" as he made his way along the bush track; then there was "a long walk over hot sand" before "the headland turned into cliffs," which meant "a 40-minute scramble," and only then was the "hidden stretch of beach...exposed."

At the shoreline, any number of obstacles can stand between the surfer and the break: vertical cliffs pounded ceaselessly by waves; rock platforms with jagged, flesh-tearing pits and protrusions; boulders covered in slippery seaweed and algal blooms; coral reefs inhabited by stonefish. When touched, the stout spines on the dorsal fin of a stonefish eject toxic venom; in serious cases the venom produces "intense pain, difficulty breathing, shock, coma, cardiac arrest and death" (Wolf 2000, 63).

On rocky shorelines, entry into the surf can require perfect timing and skill. John Grissim, a former contributing editor to *Surfing,* recalls his poorly executed launch from the rock platform at Whale Beach (Sydney). Grissim managed to "advance a mere forty feet" from the platform before a wave lumbered toward him. When he realized that the wave might hurl him into the rocks he pushed his board away:

As I broke out of the white water, I saw the wave toss my board high in the air, sending it cartwheeling end over end onto the ledge. I was now twenty feet from the rocks, firmly in the grasp of the rip, and scared shitless. Another wave broke over me, and yet another, each time pushing me another five feet closer to the rocks. A few more and I would be picked up and pitched bodily against a wall of jagged volcanic rock, [and] probably knocked unconscious. (Grissim 1982, 49)

Luckily, Grissim managed to hold his position until a friend towed him out of the rip and harm's way.

Many surfers confine their entry into the water to sandy shorelines. But even here, hazards can threaten. It took Greg Noll and Mike Stange over an hour to paddle through the shorebreak (waves that break close to, or directly on, the beach) at Pipeline during one large swell in 1964. After watching the surf for a while, the pair observed a place where

> an incoming current hit the lateral current and formed a saddle, a slot where we might be able to take advantage of the current and shoot through the shorebreak. Trouble was, we had to start about three hundred yards up from this spot and drift along with the current, timing it just right so that we'd be sucked out through the slot rather than dumped back on the sand. We got dumped at least four times before we made it out. (Noll and Gabbard 1989, 137)

Almost invariably, as the surf increases in size, so too do levels of anxiety. "When the surf gets really big," says Greg Noll, "all [the] bullshit—laughing, joking, giving each other a hard time—goes out the window. [The] guys' attitudes change. Peter Cole would get a little more hyper, Buzzy Trent would start talking faster, Pat Curren would go quieter. I'd start hyperventilating extra loud" (Noll and Gabbard 1989, 4–5). Big-surf conditions—roaring winds, constant motion, eye-burning salty spray, thundering waves, loose rocks grinding along the ocean floor—assault the senses and magnify the anxiety. Renowned big-wave rider Brock Little says he usually feels "calm and mellow" on the beach at Waimea Bay until he starts paddling and "realize[s] what I'm getting into." "When humongous waves move in," he adds, "I feel anticipation run across my entire body" (Little 1989, 112 and 113). Anxiety is particularly intense if the surfer is riding a break for the first time. Brad Gerlach, who finished second in the inaugural Tow-in World Cup in 2002 with his partner Mike Parsons, vividly recalls his first encounter with the big-wave colossus Jaws (Maui, see chapter 4) and feeling like "a deer in headlights" (*Making the Call* 2003, ch. 4).

In large surf, many surfers begin their session by catching relatively smaller waves in order to "build some momentum" until "they feel almost invincible.... At that point it doesn't matter what wave you catch," says renowned big-wave rider Shane Dorian, "you feel like you're going to make it" (Doherty 2008, 29th moment). However, such is the surge of endorphins in some surfers (see chapter 3) that they skip the warm-up. "You wanna small one to start?" Laird Hamilton asked Koby Abberton during a session in 20-foot waves at Cloudbreak: "F**k no," Abberton replied, adding, "tow me in to the biggest one you can find, as deep as you can get me." On the very next set Abberton "backdoored" his biggest barrel ever (Doherty 2008, 76th moment). Abberton notwithstanding, most surfers, especially those paddling-in to large waves, play cat and mouse with the waves.

Professional surfer Dean Morrison offers a classic example of this game. With 10-footers breaking on the second reef at Pipeline, Morrison paddled into smaller waves on the first reef between sets: "You just had to wait for a big set to roll through, then paddle your arse off to the inside and try to pick one of these off before another set rolled through. Get in, get out. You couldn't sit in there or you'd get a big second reef set on the head" (Doherty 2008, 64th moment).

The primary hazards in big surf are the sheer power and force in the waves and the topography of the seabed underneath. Greg Noll compares entanglement in a collapsing 35-foot wall of water with "going off Niagara Falls without the barrel." He estimates the chances of drowning at "about eighty percent" (Noll and Gabbard 1989, 5). After his widely publicized wipeout at Maverick's in 1994, Jay Moriarty spoke of having the "skin ripped" off his body (Warshaw 2000, 14–15). The most common causes of entanglement are wiping out (falling from the surfboard while riding a wave), a mis-timed exit from a wave, and getting caught inside a breaking wave or a closeout set. Any number of factors can cause a wipeout, although generally surfers are most vulnerable on a steep/late paddle-in take-off.

Exiting from a wave is also a delicate maneuver. The surfer who decides to leave a wave—probably because it is closing out—usually drives toward the feathering crest. However, often riders find themselves too late or ill-positioned for this option and will "straighten out" (i.e., head directly toward the shore in the same direction as the wave) to avoid the guillotine lip and the full concentration of the breaking wave.

Towed-in to one wave at Jaws in 2002, Brad Gerlach released the rope just as it peaked "a football field in front" of him. He managed to straighten out but was still engulfed by tons of white water. Gerlach compared the encounter to standing on the end of a "teeter-totter [seesaw] and someone jumping from two stories on to the other end and being suddenly sent baa boom into space." Compounding the hazard was the fact that Gerlach's entanglement occurred on the first wave of a four-wave set, with each of the following waves dragging him deeper into the swash. Gerlach's partner attempted to rescue him; Gerlach missed the sled on the first pass (a sled attaches to personal watercraft and is used in rescues; see chapter 6), although he did manage to grab the rope—briefly: the half-submerged Gerlach had to release his lifeline as water rushed through his nose (*Making the Call* 2003, ch. 4).

Guillotined: Jamie Gordon hit by the full force of a thick lip. The Island (New Zealand), 2004. *Source:* Mark Stevenson.

No matter how experienced, all surfers eventually confront entanglement with a wave that breaks on or in front of them while they are paddling. Sometimes the surfer will paddle fast and try to slip under the guillotine lip and push through the breaking wall. In April 2000 Briece Taerea tried this on a 25-foot wall of water at Teahupo'o (Tahiti). But the wave at the world's most challenging and dangerous reef (see chapter 4) was too thick; it repelled him, ramming his body into the seabed and breaking his neck and back. Taerea died two days later (Warshaw 2004, 633).

More often, the surfer is able to dive safely under the oncoming wall. Even this can be dangerously tiring when closeout sets comprise multiple waves. Brock Little confronted seven consecutive closeout waves in one session at Waimea Bay:

> [A] huge, black, monstrous wave, lined up end to end across the Bay, covering the horizon, about to closeout. [I]t broke right in front of me. I figure the thing was 32–35 feet. I took two or three deep breaths, then slid off my board. When I came up I was feeling so good that when I saw one more, it didn't bother me. I took another deep breath. Up from wave number two, though, I saw another closeout. I was still pretty comfortable.... I hadn't really taken a full-on breath because I was feeling too cocky after the first couple of waves—but now I

> **death** "It's not tragic to die doing something you love. It's like the shuttle astronauts. [W]hen they died . . . they were doing what they had geared their whole lives to do. They were at the climax of that, and it's not a bad way to go. If you want the ultimate thrill, you've got to be willing to pay the ultimate price" (Mark Foo, *Surfer*, February 1987: 63).

realized I'd been washed onto a sandbar near the middle of the Bay. [A]ll the white water had been rejuvenated when it struck the sandbar, and it was taking its newfound energy out on me. I was tired when I surfaced but doing okay. The fourth wave worked me harder than the third one—I was really fighting for air. I still wasn't in any real trouble after I came up. . . . I began taking deep breaths for wave number five. I thought I was ready for the fifth wave, but I wasn't. [A]fter a couple of seconds I started fighting, which . . . just caused my body to lose oxygen. When I came up again I saw another huge wave. I did everything right: took a deep breath, didn't panic, and started fighting after about five seconds. The seventh wave barely closed out the Bay. I went under and prayed this was the last wave of the set. When I came up I was about 30 yards from shore. (Little 1989, 141)

Despite oxygen starvation, Little had the presence of mind to swim to the middle of the bay and recover his breath rather than head shoreward immediately. He then swam into smaller waves, which pushed him to within 25 yards of the shore. Only then did he expend the last of his energy to fight his way to the beach (Little 1989, 142).

Turbulence and pressure are not the only hazards in an entanglement. The surfer's board can also transform into a deadly projectile. Titus Kinimaka felt the full impact of a free-floating surfboard during a wipeout in 15- to 18-foot surf at Waimea Bay in 1989. Exploding white water catapulted his board into his thigh "like a knife-edge" and snapped his femur in two (Kinimaka 2008). Kimo Hollinger collided with his board when a six-foot lip at Pupukea (O'ahu) "guillotined" him. The fin slashed deep into Hollinger's right thigh, narrowly missing his femoral artery. Assisted by a fellow surfer, it took Hollinger 10 minutes to return to shore; he would have died in 2 had the important artery been severed (Grissim 1982, 5).

The death of Briece Taerea, to which I referred above, confirms the hazards posed by the seabed. Surfers riding in shallow water over coral reefs

Dangerous "signs": A nasty lip about to detonate on a very shallow reef, with Mike Tehana between the two. The Island (New Zealand), 2005. *Source:* Mark Stevenson.

often find perfect tubes, but they also risk some of the heaviest wipeouts. When Heath Walker hit the reef at Off The Wall (Oʻahu), he was knocked out and suffered a broken collarbone, broken ribs, and a punctured lung, and his left ear was almost severed (Doherty 2008, 50th moment). Surfers must be able to read the marine topography, which is not always easy. "Sometimes," says Nat Young (1998, 395), the signs that usually mark shallower water over a reef, such as a boil on the face of the wave, are absent and "the wave just sucks out revealing dry reef."

Rocks protruding from reefs are also common obstacles at surf breaks. Renowned big-wave rider Justen "Jughead" Allport vividly recalls encountering an obstacle rock at an unnamed reef in Western Australia. At this reef the rock protrudes three feet out of the open ocean in front of the wave, and on this occasion Allport collided with it after a wipeout:

I . . . just plunged straight down into deep water on the other side of it. I've come back up and thought, thank f**k that's over, I took one breath then this 5-foot backwash that'd wrapped around the rock picked me up and threw me back in front of the rock again, just as another set's coming. It hits me and I'm on the rock again for the third time, but thankfully it washes me to the side. (Doherty 2008, 26th moment)

Deep holes formed by coral polyps also pose unique dangers, as legendary big-wave rider Jose Angel discovered. After wiping out on a 15-foot wave at Pipeline in 1967, Angel was "blasted" by the exploding turbulence into a pitch-black vertical cavern with an overhanging lip. Disoriented, he searched in vain for the exit. He escaped only when a subsequent wave broke particularly hard on the reef and the release of energy literally ejected him from a potential coral coffin (Wolf 2000, 81–82; see also Van Dyke 1988, 95–96).

Tow-in surfing fundamentally changed the relationship between surfers by introducing support teams and teamwork (see chapter 2). Traditionally, surfers emphasized their individuality and relied totally on their own skills. They never expected help from others. Indeed, when Mark Foo drowned after wiping out on a relatively small 15-foot wave at Maverick's, his body floated for two hours before being discovered, despite the fact that a photographer had captured his last wave and wipeout on film. Of course, in monstrous waves surfers without technological assistance are simply unable to help their peers in trouble. After Greg Noll wiped out at Makaha in 1969, his close friend and local lifeguard, Richard "Buffalo" Keaulana, tracked his movements in the water. But all Keaulana could offer Noll when the latter finally heaved himself onto the beach was, "good ting you wen make 'em Brudda, 'cause no way I was comin' in afta you. I was jus goin' wave goodbye and say 'Alooo-ha'" (Noll and Gabbard 1989, 9). By contrast, assistance is an integral element of tow-in surfing; riders now expect their drivers to risk their lives and the equipment to collect partners trapped in the impact zone (see chapter 2).

Finally, at some point the surfer decides to return to land. Sometimes this can be the most hazardous of all journeys. Captain James King, who assumed command of the *Resolution* after the death of explorer James Cook in 1779, recorded the dangers faced by early Hawai'ian surfers in leaving the water:

Those who succeed in their object of reaching shore, have still the greatest danger to encounter. The coast being guarded by a chain of rocks, with, here and there, a small opening between them, they are obliged to steer their boards through one of these, or, in case of failure, to quit it, before they reach the rocks, and, plunging under the wave, make the best of their way back again. (cited in Marcus 2008, 9–10)

In a more contemporary setting, Corb Donohue recounts a lone dawn surf in a rising swell at Kawela Bay (O'ahu). Hit by a 12-foot closeout, Donohue lost his board and began the 1-mile swim to the beach:

> Twenty minutes later I was pretty exhausted and nearing the point that separates Kawela Bay from Turtle Bay, when I suddenly saw I was in real trouble: the wave surge was carrying me across a shallow reef toward a strong rip that would suck me deep into the razor-sharp lava undercuts of the point. Twenty feet closer to the shore and I'd be dead. At that instant I realized that absolutely no one was going to take care of this for me.... The fear was horrible, paralyzing. I felt nauseous—but no sooner had I understood it was swim hard or die than the fear passed and I snapped into intense focus. I no longer had spaghetti arms, strength returned from somewhere, and as I swam diagonally across the incoming white water, every muscle and nerve in me strained to move out two hundred feet [on to the sands of Turtle Bay]. (Grissim 1982, 47–48)

Of course, among aficionados land is only a temporary space in between sessions.

Having outlined the cultural dimensions of extreme surfing and the physical risks, I will now provide more detail of selected elements, beginning with the history of big-wave riding.

2. origins

There is a wild burst of foam, a long tumultuous rushing sound as the breaker falls futile and spent on the beach;...and there at your feet steps calmly ashore a Kanaka....He has "bitted the bull-mouthed breaker" and ridden it in, and the pride in the feat shows in the carriage of his magnificent body as he glances for a moment carelessly at you....He is...a member of the kingly species that has mastered matter and the brutes and lorded it over creation. And one sits and thinks...that Kanaka...knows [the] joy of the sea...and what that Kanaka can do, you can do yourself....And that is how it came about that I tackled surf-riding.

Jack London (1911, 68–69)

extreme surfing has a long history, with ancient Hawaiʻian legends extolling the feats of big-wave riders. Most modern accounts of extreme surfing date from the mid-20th century as riders ventured to Oʻahu in growing numbers, first to the breaks on the South Shore at Waikiki (between Diamond Head and Ala Wai Yacht Harbor), then west to Makaha and then to the North Shore. Importantly, photography and film corroborated many of the personal heroics and eyewitness accounts. In the early 1990s, towing riders into waves that were impossible to catch by paddling thrust surfing into a new realm of extreme. In this chapter I recount the history of big-wave surfing in the 20th century and the more recent development of tow-in surfing. This chapter is not a definitive history. Rather, I offer a narrative of those events, people, and memories that, in the words of John Long (1999, 5), "refused to be excluded" and "sparked a special excitement."

This approach captures much of the fervent passion of surfing's devotees and their indefatigable quest to discover new breaks and to ride steeper, bigger, and more hollow waves. It is an approach that tends to overemphasize "firsts" and that typically ignores antecedents. The claim by Phil Edwards that he was the first to ride Pipeline is a classic example:

> For twenty years people have been saying to me, "You weren't the first. Some Ancient Hawaiian king probably rode it on a log centuries ago." Well, f**k them: I was the first [in mid-December 1961]. I dragged a bunch of guys down there that day. I wanted someone to hold my hand and I admit it. They all had the chance. They were all tougher guys than me. I don't claim to be a macho man, but I did it and they didn't so there. (Moses 1982, 95)

Such accounts and claims are not necessarily falsehoods or fabrications, but they are mostly highly selective versions of the past, produced and created at the expense of alternative accounts (Osmond and Phillips 2006, 44; see also Martin 2009) and usually devoid of context. Fred Hemmings (1997, 53) says he rode Pipeline in 1960, although he admits his solitary wave during that session ended in a nasty wipeout and he acknowledges Edwards as "the first modern-day surfer to successfully ride the Pipeline." However, George Downing, whom surfing historian Matt Warshaw knights "the original big-wave surfer," the man who built the first specialized big-wave surfboards and led explorations of many North Shore breaks (*Riding Giants* 2004, ch. 4; Warshaw 2004, 162–64), offers a broader and deeper perspective. Skeptical of the idea of firsts, Downing refers to ancient Hawai'ian "footprints on waves" (Parmenter 1999, 94):

> With the knowledge the Hawaiians had, with their energies and abilities as watermen, I cannot imagine that they didn't ride waves I've been privileged to ride myself. Every time we felt we were on to something new in design, we found it already in the Hawaiian boards. We knew nothing....

One doesn't have to look far to find examples of selective history in surfing. Australian Bernard "Midget" Farrelly was a major figure in world surfing throughout the 1960s. He won the Makaha International in 1962, the inaugural World Championship in 1964 and the prestigious Gunston 500 in South Africa in 1970. He placed second in the 1968 and 1970 world titles and contributed to the revolution in surfboard design that occurred in the 1960s. Yet, after he lost the world title to fellow Australian Robert "Nat" Young in 1966, the surf media essentially wrote Farrelly out of history, consigning him to "yesterday's news" and "generally made him unwelcome in what [it] billed as the 'New Era' " of shortboard surfing (Warshaw 2004, 193–94; Jarratt 2007). Other conspicuous examples include the omissions of big-wave pioneer George Downing from Nat Young's *The History of Surfing* (1983) and pioneer tow-in surfer Burton "Buzzy" Kerbox from *Strapped: The Origins of Tow-in Surfing* (2002). And while total fabrications may be rare, embellishments are common. History has all but forgotten Ken Bradshaw's outstanding performance in closeout surf at Waimea Bay on January 18, 1985. By contrast, Mark Foo did not complete a single wave that day and was eventually pulled from the ocean by a helicopter (see chapter 6). Yet, Foo's account of the session, which he sent to surf magazines, secured him legend status (Warshaw 1995b, 109).

The stories of discoveries and firsts that dominate the history of surfing often imply causation, which, of course, is implicit in the very word "history." But historians are notoriously poor at proving precise causes; historians of surfing are no different. In the previous chapter, for example, I referred to an assault on Nat Young. What caused the assault: why did a fellow surfer, Michael Hutchinson, viciously attack Young? In one sense, the cause appears uncontested: Young dropped-in on a wave "claimed" by a friend of Michael's son Luke, who responded with a stream of obscenities directed at the older surfer. Young responded, in his words (Young 2000, 17–18), by "swatting" Luke "in the mouth in the way you would smack a puppy when it does the wrong thing," and this provoked Michael. But was it *the* cause? Perhaps not. Earlier the same day, Young's son, Beau, dropped-in on Hutchinson, who at the end of the wave cast a hostile glare toward the young surfer. The glare drew a verbal reaction from the senior Young, who had observed the incident: "Don't worry about Michael 'cause he does that to everyone." According to Young, "Michael kept paddling" but "I could feel him seething." Were Young's words *the* cause of the assault? Perhaps not. Young describes years of frosty relations between the pair that he attributes to Hutchinson's use of his longboard to dominate Angourie surf, which Young said violates one of "the unspoken rules of surfing." Young usually responded to Hutchinson by "leaving the water whenever he paddled out." But in retrospect this only "pissed off" Hutchinson. Was Young's strategy of avoidance *the* cause of the assault in 2000? We'll never know. And this leads directly to my point. Historians typically imply causation simply by starting their narrative at one particular point—a drop-in, a swat in the mouth, leaving the water. In short, the assault raises a series of questions that remind historians that they choose when and where they begin their story and these choices are matters of their own biases, judgments, and interpretations rather than grounded in some higher truth.

Likewise, historians make judgments about the context in which they place events and people. As I alluded to in the previous chapter, historians of big-wave surfing have largely confined their contexts to hedonistic lifestyles and fratriarchal relationships. While perfectly valid, these contexts nonetheless tend to romanticize surfing. Photographs of "grinning faces," stripped torsos, and "clutters of balsa surfboards, wine jugs and peanut butter jars" may suggest that surfers found paradise at Makaha in the early 1950s, but not all were happy and content. Philip "Flippy" Hoffman described an "awful" three months at Makaha in the winter of 1952–53: "I had boils and carbuncles all over. Dysentery—we were all really f****d up" (Warshaw 2000, 31, 34). In the early 1980s, Gerry Lopez, who is often referred to as the King of Pipeline, used sarcasm to mock the romanticization of big-wave riding in popular tales of the sport:

> There was a time when big wave surfing was the only way to gain admission into Surfing Valhalla—the Place of Eternal Surfing—where you surf to win or die on enormous waves all day long—getting fantastic rides—thirty-minute nose rides, longer tube rides, left sliders, rights, everything, anything, hideous wipeouts that hold you down for hours and dash you on reefs tearing you from limb to limb but somehow you are always made whole again for the nights with the best parties with the most beautiful surfer girls..., kegs of beer, wine, carrot juice—whatever you want—fabulous buffets, dope, music, surf movies, everything.... But only for those who have led the life of a true surfer where honor and valor are the true measure and the big, high, scary waves are the means by which one can hope for a seat within the Halls of Valhalla. (Brady 1983, 42 and 44)

Judging from much of the contemporary literature, this romanticism remains.

ancient hawai'i

Among the legends of big-wave riding feats in Hawai'ian culture are the stories of Holoua, Māmala, Kahikilani, Kelea, Hauailiki, and Umi-a-līloa. Holoua lived near the water on Kaua'i. When the first wave in a set of tsunami washed him, his house, and all of his belongings out to sea, he pulled

---

ancient surfboards   Premodern Hawai'ian boardmakers
produced *olo* and *alaia* boards. Olo boards were used exclu-
sively by chiefs; they were 14½ to 18 feet long, 16 to 24 inches
wide, and 5 to 8 inches thick. Alaia boards were 7 to 12 feet
long, 13 to 20 inches wide, and much thinner at ½ to 1½ inches.
Both forms had mildly convex top and bottom decks tapering
to rounded rails; neither had fins. They were made from wiliwili,
koa, or breadfruit trees. Boardmakers shaped the basic design
with stone and bone adzes and then smoothed the surfaces with
granulated coral and 'oahi stone. They stained the boards with
juices from the roots, bark, and seeds of local plants, and sealed
them with oil extracted from kukui nuts.

---

a plank from the side of his house. He used this to ride the next wave in the
set, a 50-footer, back to the shore (Finney and Houston 1996, 76).

A kupua (a demigod or hero with supernatural powers who could assume various forms including a beautiful woman, a gigantic lizard, and a
great shark), Māmala was a prominent O'ahu chief and highly skilled surfer
who rode the roughest waves that broke beyond the harbor area of Honolulu, far out to sea. She drew "resounding applause" from her people, who
"clapped their hands over her extraordinary athletic feats" (Gault-Williams
2008). The area Māmala surfed became known as Ke-kai-o-Māmala (Sea
of Māmala), which includes the well-known contemporary surf breaks of
Ala Moana, Rock Pile, In-betweens, and Kaisers (Gault-Williams 2008).

Kahikilani, a prince from Kaua'i, crossed a hundred miles of open sea
between his home and O'ahu to ride the giant waves of Paumalu (Sunset
Beach).

As he rode he was watched by a bird maiden with supernatural powers who lived in a cave on a nearby mountain. She fell in love with
the prince and sent bird messengers to place an orange lehua lei
around his neck and bring him to her. By flying around his head, the
messengers guided Kahikilani to the bird maiden's cave. Enchanted,
he spent several months with her, until the return of the surfing season. Then the distant sizzle and boom of the waves at Paumalu were
too much for Kahikilani to resist, and he left the maiden, but only after
promising never to kiss another woman. However, the excitement

of the rising surf must have clouded his memory because almost as soon as he was riding again, a beautiful woman came walking along the white sand. She saw him there, waited until he rode to shore, placed an ilima lei around his neck, and kissed him. His vow was broken. He thought nothing of it and paddled back out to the breaking waves, but the bird messengers were watching. They flew to tell their mistress of his infidelity. When she heard their report, the bird maiden ran to the beach with a lehua lei in her hand. Snatching the ilima lei from Kahikilani's neck, she replaced it with the one made from lehua blossoms. As she ran back to her cave, he chased her. That was the last Kahikilani saw of the bird maiden, though, for halfway up the mountain he was turned to stone. (Finney and Houston 1996, 35)

Known as an unforgiving chief, Umi-a-līloa ruled over the islands of Hawai'i and Maui in the late 15th and early 16th centuries. Around 1480, Umi, then a prince, and a friend attended a surf riding competition incognito at Laupahoehoe, near Hilo. Upon arrival, Umi declared that he excelled at surfing, a claim that a lesser chief but skilled surfer named Paiea viewed with skepticism. Paiea challenged Umi to surf against him at a difficult break in front of Laupahoehoe for a purse of four double-hulled canoes. Different accounts of the contest record different victors; some claim Paiea won, others Umi. Regardless of which version one believes, they all conclude with Umi rising to power as high chief and returning, several years later, to Hilo, where he had Paiea killed and sacrificed to his god (Gault-Williams 2008).

Irrespective of the factual content of these stories, each of them carries important messages, not least that surfing is as much a social activity as an individual pursuit and that honor and truth are integral to those relationships. These ideas, touched on in the preceding chapter, resurface in the following narratives of big-wave surfing in the 20th century and help frame conclusions about the nature of extreme surfing.

"once-in-a-lifetime ride"   **In the summer of 1917, Duke Kahanamoku, the patron saint of surfing, claimed "the ride to end all rides" (Kahanamoku and Brennan 1972, 80; see also Brennan 1994, 125–26) at Waikiki. Using a 114-pound, 16-foot board, Kahanamoku rode a wave that peaked at over 20 feet from Outside Castles to the shoreline at Queens, a distance of 1¾ miles.**

modern oʻahu

Surfers from California began traveling to the South Shore of Oʻahu to ride big waves as early as the 1930s. Sometimes they encountered more than they had bargained for. California lifeguard Tom Zahn vividly recalls his first session in the summer of 1942. Within half an hour of his entering the water at Queens, the surf had risen from 6 to 12 feet and Zahn found himself in the "vortex" of First Break confronting "giant, unpredictable walls of water." Looking to catch a small wave back to shore, Zahn scanned the horizon to see what, at first glance, he thought was a bank of fog. Zahn then realized he was looking at a rogue wall of water that filled the horizon: "I...had a sudden rush of [adrenaline] and then I felt a chill from head to toe. It looked that big. My stomach jumped up and lodged somewhere in my throat" (Wolf 2000, 8–9).

Zahn now confronted the surfer's perennial dilemma: should he paddle toward the wave in the hope of passing over the feathering crest or at least punch through the wall? Or should he turn and paddle shoreward and hope that the broken wave would diffuse most of its energy before engulfing him? Already a noted paddler who would go on to win the 32-mile Catalina-Manhattan race four times, Zahn opted for the former, rising to his knees and sprinting for the horizon. At the base of the wave, and partly "blinded by the spray," Zahn shut his eyes, wrapped himself around his board, and "hoped for the best":

> I must have broken through [the wall] at the last instant, just before the wave took hold of my board and threw me out. I expected a big drop down the backside but I wasn't ready for what a Hawaiian offshore wind can do to a big wave. When I did break through I shot into the air like a rocket. The wave crashed behind me and the sound of it echoed like stacking timbers. I must have shot fifteen feet through the air on the backside of that wave. In fact the backside was bigger than the front of any wave I'd ever ridden. I turned over mid-air and, luckily, I was able to hold on to my board. (Wolf 2000, 10–11)

Lady Luck continued to smile on Zahn; the following waves were smaller and all broke shoreward. The swell, however, remained large and Zahn decided to paddle to Diamond Head to catch a smaller wave on the inside. He finally returned to the beach after three hours.

Some surfers traveled to the west side of Oʻahu to ride bigger and faster waves at Makaha. John Kelly, Wally Froiseth, and Fran Heath from

Honolulu began making this journey in the late 1930s (Warshaw 2004, 253) and from there they explored the North Shore, even occasionally venturing into the water (Warshaw 2000, 34). One of the first recorded attempts to ride big surf on the North Shore ended in tragedy. On December 22, 1943, Woodbridge "Woody" Brown and Dickie Cross decided to try their luck in rising 10-foot surf at Sunset Beach. Shortly after entering the water they were half a mile from shore amid 25-foot waves. The pair decided to paddle three miles to Waimea Bay in the expectation of reaching the shore via a deep-water channel. At the bay they found the channel impassable. As big-wave pioneer and oceanographer Ricky Grigg explains, when Waimea closes out

> rip currents turn into rivers too strong to swim against. The only way to get to shore...is to swim in hugging the right side of the bay....If you drifted left toward the middle of the bay, a rip current tearing out to sea would greet you. In minutes it would transport you back outside the lineup on the far west corner of the bay. The only way to get in was another round trip, but this time hugging the whitewater. (Grigg 1998, 32)

Cross and Brown lost their boards in successive closeout sets. Brown did not see Cross again when he resurfaced after diving deep to avoid a closeout wave. Brown returned to shore following the "lifeline" of whitewater, as fellow big-wave pioneer Charles "Buzzy" Trent called it (Grigg 1998, 32). Thrashed to exhaustion by some dozen waves en route, a "barely conscious" Brown (1993, 87) "crawled up the beach." His "harrowing tale kept surfers away from the area for a few years" (Warshaw 2004, 88, 141, and 677). Brown continued to ride Makaha, taking up winter residence there with other California surfers in the early 1950s; he occasionally returned to the North Shore "but never with the same old fire" (Brown 1993, 87).

Brown and his Makaha companions, however, who included Buzzy Trent, Jim Fisher, Walter Hoffman, and Honolulu locals George Downing and Wally Froiseth, constituted the "first really hard core big-wave riders" who "set the blueprint for the next generation" (Greg Noll cited in *Riding Giants* 2004, ch. 4). Surf journalist Dave Parmenter (1999, 92 and 94) likens them to Himalayan mountaineers, test pilots, and "heroic frontiersmen" (see also Parmenter 1987, 93). In 1953 a photograph of Brown, Downing, and Trent racing across a 15-foot wall at Makaha appeared in newspapers across the United States. The photograph inspired a new generation of surfers (Warshaw 2004, 88).

George Downing, Woody Brown, and Buzzy Trent, Makaha, December 1953. This widely published photograph enticed many surfers to Oʻahu. *Source:* AP Photo.

At the end of the 1950s some California surfers searching for big waves moved to Hawaiʻi permanently; dozens of others visited in winter (Warshaw 2004, 253–54). In 1957 Greg Noll led Pat Curren, Mickey Muñoz, Fred Van Dyke, Bing Copeland, Del Cannon, Harry Church, Bob Bermel, and Mike Stange into 15-foot waves at Waimea. "I remember paddling into that lineup," Noll says, and "my balls were in my stomach, thinking that the bottom was going to fall out and something was going to eat me alive" (*Riding Giants* 2004, ch. 5). Waimea would be the epicenter of big-wave surfing for the next 30 years until the discovery of Maverick's in Northern California and the emergence of tow-in surfing in the early 1990s.

Surfing underwent a transformation in the 1970s as shortboards redefined the notion of high performance, and Waimea gave way to Pipeline and Sunset as tuberiding became the measure of surfing excellence. Surfers also formed a professional circuit in this decade, and the magazines turned their attention to "small wave ripping and the 'surf stars' on the pro-tour." Professional surfing, said big-wave rider Alec "Ace Cool"

Cooke, is "where the money and sponsors are, and the sponsors support the magazines...so that's what the magazines cover" (Brady 1983, 42). Ken Bradshaw attributes the decline in big-wave riding to the lull in swells (see chapter 3). There have been "a few decent sized days" since 1977, Bradshaw said in 1983,

> but they've just been too big for Sunset and too small for Waimea. Fifteen to eighteen [feet] is not Waimea. And the five or six times it got twenty [feet], it was blown out! '77 was the last good year for big waves. (Brady 1983, 48)

In 1983 surfing journalist Leonard Brady challenged the surfing fraternity with a set of provocative questions: why are only a handful of riders "scrambling for the baddest of the biggest set waves?" "Have surfers turned into candy asses? Is surfing now a viable alternative to general wimpdom? Will lavender be the board color of the eighties?" (Brady 1983, 40). Brady noted only three big-wave surfers at the time: Clyde Aikau, James Jones, and Ken Bradshaw. But the waning of interest in pursuing monster waves was only temporary.

Like Bradshaw, surfing historian Matt Warshaw (2004, 620) credits the reemergence of big-wave riding to the swell of 1983 (see chapter 3); Warshaw also notes the role of the second Eddie Aikau memorial contest (see chapters 4 and 5) held in 1987, which refocused attention on Waimea Bay. The leading exponents in the second era of big-wave surfing were Jeff Hakman, Jock Sutherland, Eddie and Clyde Aikau, Nat Young, Mark Richards, Ian Cairns, Mike Doyle, Barry Kanaiaupuni, Gerry Lopez, James Jones, Reno Abellira, and Shaun Tomson.

---

professor grigg   Surfer Ricky Grigg graduated with a BS from Stanford University in 1958, a MS from the University of Hawai'i (1970), and a PhD in oceanography from the Scripps Institution of Oceanography (University of California–San Diego, 1970). He joined the faculty in the Department of Oceanography at the University of Hawai'i in 1970 and became a world authority on the ecology of coral reefs. In 1980 Grigg discovered Darwin Point, the latitude at the northwestern end of Hawai'i where the island chain "drowns."

Ricky Grigg (1998, 34) believes this group was "more athletic than their...forebears." However, this era would pale in comparison with the dimensions of big-wave riding ushered in by tow-in surfing. Comparing the feats of his generation to contemporary big-wave riders, Greg Noll declared that we were just "a bunch of guys paddling around on rubber duckies in a kiddie pool" (Weisberg 2009).

tow-in surfing

Stories of surfers using motorized craft to tow-in to waves breaking on offshore reefs date from the 1970s, although even here the ancient Hawai'ian practice of *lele wa'a,* canoe leaping, offers something of a precedent; in *lele wa'a* surfers leapt with their board from the prow of a canoe into a cresting wave (Parmenter 1999, 94). Jeff Johnson, Flippy Hoffman, Roger Erickson, and David Kahanamoku used a 24-foot skiff with outboard motors to tow-in at Avalanche (off-shore from Haleiwa Harbor) in the mid-1970s (Jenkins 1993, 50). In 1987, during a lay day at the Pipeline Masters contest, Herbie Fletcher used a personal watercraft (PWC)—then used by lifeguards to perform rescues in big seas (see chapter 6)—to tow-in Martin Potter and Tom Carroll at second reef Pipeline; Potter rode one wave through to the inside, which ended in a classic tube. Recalling the wave some years later, renowned bodyboarder and lifeguard Mark Cunningham said, "I felt we were seeing the future that day, and I was almost afraid to see who'd be out there the following winter. But it never caught on" (Jenkins 1993, 50 and 52). In 1992 Laird Hamilton and Buzzy Kerbox used a Zodiac (a motorized inflatable boat) to tow-in to 16-foot waves at Sunset. Hamilton and Kerbox then took the idea to Maui, where they owned property, and where they interacted with a group of extreme windsurfers who were already playing at Pe'ahi ("beckon") (later named Jaws), literally sailing into giant waves (Lopez 1995, 94 and 98).

At Jaws, which Hamilton describes as "five Waimeas" (*Riding Giants* 2004, ch. 23), the technology of tow-in surfing developed rapidly with the introduction of shortboards that combined features of snowboards, water skis, and surfboards, and included footstraps. The short tow-in board was the real breakthrough, says Hamilton, enabling us to "shift gear: now we suddenly had speed" (*Riding Giants* 2004, ch. 21). Speed is necessary both to catch large waves (water moves up the face of a wave like a treadmill and on waves over 30 feet will often be traveling faster than the surfer can paddle-in to the wall) and to skip around sections previously impossible

to make on a paddle-in board (Jenkins 1993, 50). Surfing history now ac-
knowledges the "Strapped Crew"—Mark Angulo, Pete Cabrinha, Darrick
Doerner, Laird Hamilton, Dave Kalama, Brett Lickle, Rush Randle, and
Mike Waltze—as the founders of tow-in surfing (*Strapped* 2002).

While the Strapped Crew produced and distributed videos of their exploits at Jaws, a segment in Bruce Brown's *The Endless Summer II* (1994)
catapulted tow-in surfing into the mainstream of big-wave riding. The
film's Hollywood backers also provided the surfers with a Yamaha Wave-
Runner for towing-in (*The Endless Summer II* 1994, ch. 13) and in so
doing cemented the place of the PWC as the preferred tow-in vehicle. As
well as being faster and more maneuverable than the Zodiac, PWC were
safer, using a water propulsion system rather than an outboard motor with
a potentially deadly spinning propeller (Lopez 1995, 98).

However, tow-in surfing sparked intense debate. Critics, including Ken
Bradshaw, called tow-in surfers "phonies" and labeled the practice "cheat-
ing" on the grounds that it removed the single most difficult aspect of
paddle-in big-wave riding, namely the "take-off and drop" (e.g., Warshaw
2000, 154). Dave Parmenter sums up the critics' arguments:

> Did you ever see the movie *Hatari*? They're hunting rhinos in Kenya
> and they have this special truck with a seat on the hood, and as they
> go alongside the rhino at 50 mph, the guy in front drags him with a
> noose. To me surfing is having the rhino charge *you,* and you're there
> by yourself in a pair of trunks. It's Greg Noll, a solitary guy facing his
> ultimate fear, and here comes a big black one around the point. You
> have to choke back that fear, turn around, match the speed of the
> wave and choke over that ledge. These tow-in guys have the truck,
> and they're chasing right along with the rhino, at its speed. They're
> going faster than the wave right off the bat. Plus it's motors and noise,
> the smell of octane—that doesn't appeal to me at all. And this extreme
> surfing, you've got to have a partnership, your gear, your walkie-talkies.
> I've never thought of surfing as teamwork. (Jenkins 1997, 111)

Big-wave legend Brock Little likens tow-in surfing to "riding on a roller
coaster" while paddling-in to big waves is more comparable to "jumping off an 80-foot cliff." The two forms are technically quite different. In
waves over 25 feet, the surfer paddling-in must stroke strongly, efficiently,
and confidently, literally under the lip of the wave, and, even assuming
a perfectly executed take-off (i.e., with the rail of the board "grabbing"
the wall and the rider standing upright on the deck and controlling the

board), the success rate at breaks like Waimea Bay and Maverick's are "only slightly better than 50 percent" (Duane 1998a). Former world champion Sunny Garcia laments that surfers who have never even paddled-in to a 10-foot wave, let alone 20-footers, are now being towed-in to 60-foot waves. In his words, "every average Joe who can stand up on a board can get towed-in to a really big wave and claim to be a big-wave surfer... but I would say about 50 to 75 percent... are just kooks" (Bradley 2005).

Hamilton rejects these arguments. The real issue, he says, is "high performance and efficiency." Being towed-in allows the surfer to get deeper into the tube. Moreover, it means that surfers can "ride the wave twice as far *and* be back to catch another wave" quickly. Thus, it is "totally superior" with respect to both physical exertion and the actual time spent riding. In Hamilton's words, "I'm here to surf, OK? I've done enough wiping out. I want to make the wave now. Most guys think tow-in surfing is weak, or it's not manly or something, which is great. Killer. They'll just be that much farther behind when they see the light" (Jenkins 1997, 114–15).

Ken Bradshaw certainly revised his opinion. After initially blustering that surfers should "either paddle-in to the waves [under their own] power or get the hell out of the water," he conceded that towing is the "only clear-cut way to reach that next level" of riding waves over 30 feet. Bradshaw admits that towing-in eliminates a skill aspect of catching a wave, that of "locating the peak and dropping in," but he maintains "the experience is just as satisfying" (Jenkins 1993, 50). Nor does towing-in lessen the anxiety levels. Gerry Lopez describes the mere sight of Jaws as "physically nauseating." He adds that "the terror... before letting go is so great that it's a wonder no one dies of fright at that moment" (*Strapped* 2002, ch. 2). Indeed, death is a common topic of talk among big-wave surfers. On a boat at Todos Santos (Mexico) (see chapter 4) during a massive swell in 1998, journalist Daniel Duane was struck by the apparent "unflappability" of big-wave rider Evan Slater. When Duane (1998b) asked Slater how he had slept the previous night, Slater replied through an egoless smile: "You want to know the truth? I thought I was driving to my death this morning."

Tow-in surfing also transformed the individualistic nature of big-wave surfing into a partnership. New Zealand big-wave rider Daniel Kereopa articulates nicely the shared experiences that bond tow-in partners:

You're excited for yourself but you are excited for the guy who pulled you into the wave too. It's this bond, it's this love. You work together as a team for a number of years. Words don't match how you feel, you know. People do high fives but, I used to look into the eyes of my friend, and just go, "bro." He knows exactly what I'm feeling and understands the respect I have for him. It's just amazing. (Fitzjames 2009)

The shared experience of tow-in surfing also extends into a dependency relationship during rescues. "Being there in a crisis" is Hamilton's sole criterion for determining partners:

You'll never really know until you get out there. I can't tell you how many guys I thought were my friend, but when a really heavy situation came down and they didn't come and get me. . . . They didn't cross the fine line, where it goes from courage to the next level. (Jenkins 1997, 116)

Yet, the fact remains that the overwhelming majority of surfers shy away from big waves. Indeed, when the big swells arrive, excuses pour forth to explain the absences—"doctor's appointment," "collecting the kids," "work commitments," "family engagements" (Finnegan 1992, 56). Bradshaw observes that "the crowds on the beach may have increased" over

Tow-in surfing introduced new waves, new technologies and new relationships; Kyle Davidson (*left*) sharing the experience with Daniel Kereopa (*right*), Papatowai, 2006. *Source:* Mark Stevenson.

the last half-century, "but the number of guys in the water on a big day has stayed about the same" (Noll and Gabbard 1989, 147). Referring to Waimea Bay, Bradshaw notes that the only time crowds appear is when the waves break below 18 feet:

> That's when guys who want to say that they've surfed Waimea go out. They sit in the bowl area for a 15-foot wave and end up in everyone's way when a set comes through. At 18 to 20 feet, the second reef starts to pump and the crowd splits up. You get maybe 20 guys hustling for it. The first set that hits 25 foot, that's it. You're suddenly down to six or eight guys. It's that first big dark one that clears it out real fast. (Noll and Gabbard 1989, 146–47)

In the following chapter I turn attention to the science of extreme surfing. As well as discussing the physical science of big waves, including meteorology and oceanography, I also examine the biology of pleasure that helps explain why some surfers engage extreme conditions to ride monstrous waves.

3.   science

[L]et me explain the physics....A wave is a communicated agitation. The water that composes the body of a wave does not move....No, the water...is stationary. Thus, you may watch a particular portion of the ocean's surface and you will see the same water rise and fall a thousand times to the agitation communicated by a thousand successive waves. Now imagine this communicated agitation moving shoreward. As the bottom shoals, the lower portion of the wave strikes land first and is stopped. But...the upper portion has not struck anything, wherefore it keeps on communicating its agitation, keeps on going. And when the top of the wave keeps on going, while the bottom of it lags behind, something is bound to happen. The bottom of the wave drops out from under and the top of the wave falls over, forward, and down, curling and cresting and roaring as it does so. It is the bottom of a wave striking against the top of the land that is the cause of all surfs.

Jack London (1911, 69–70)

as the source of energy that propels surfers and their boards, the wave lies at the center of surfing. The prominence and breadth of language around waves in surfing culture confirms this centrality. A dozen terms describe the form of the breaking wave: left, right, A-frame, peeling, closeout, barrel, bowl, hollow, sections, fat, jacking, thick, slab, sucking, reform. Another dozen terms express the power and consistency of the wave: cooking, gnarly, heavy, mushy, firing, booming, out of control. Yet another dozen terms categorize surfing sites: shore break, beach break, point break, pier break, sandbar, wedge, bombora, bommie, reef, outer reef, offshore reef (Marcus 2008, 18–19; Cralle 2001). Surfers analyze the height of waves in microscopic detail, measuring size against their bodies—ankle-high, knee-high, waist-high, head-high, overhead, double overhead, triple over-head—and, in the case of extreme surf, "increments of fear" (Buzzy Trent cited in Cralle 2001, 317).

Behind all these terms is oceanography, the science of wave forma-tion, wave size, wave shape, and wave power. In this chapter I describe this science. Yet, while oceanography explores the primary source of en-ergy in surfing, it does not explain the obsession surfers have with riding waves. This obsession frequently assumes fanaticism, especially when measured against the length of the typical ride—which rarely extends be-yond seconds—and the risks of injury and death in extreme surf. Thus, in this chapter I also discuss the biology of surfing as a pleasure-arousing pursuit. The terms science and biology may frighten some readers; they shouldn't. Experienced surfers already possess the spirit of scientists, as Tony Butt, Paul Russell, and Rick Grigg explain:

> A surfer who spends many years waiting for, and riding, different waves in different parts of the world becomes a meteorologist, ocean-ographer, geographer, linguist and cultural expert. All that waiting, watching, discussing, waiting and thinking gives surfers an insatiable thirst for knowledge, which is typical of scientists. (Butt, Russell, and Grigg 2004, 9–10)

earth science

Waves form when winds, created by differentials in pressure and the earth's rotation, blow across oceans. The friction between air and water generates movement—ripples and waves—on the water. A gentle wind blowing between 5 and 20 kilometers per hour (about 3–12 mph) over a calm ocean surface produces waves of less than 1 centimeter (about ½ in.); fully fledged waves form when the winds strengthen to about 30 kilome-ters per hour (about 18 mph), when the winds blow for longer periods, and as the area over which the wind blows (known as fetch) increases (Grotz-inger et al. 2007, 475; Walker 1974). The single most important weather phenomenon producing waves is the low pressure system—identifiable on weather maps as closely packed isobars—which is typically at its deep-est over the sea in winter: "The deeper the depression, the faster this air moves. The faster it moves, the more it drags on the water and the bigger the waves" (Butt, Russell, and Grigg 2004, 23 and 24). Normal barometric pressure at sea level is about 1,014 millibars (29.92 in. Hg). The deepest depression on record (excluding tropical storms and tornadoes) was measured at 914 millibars (26.98 in. Hg) and occurred in the North Atlantic on January 10–11, 1993 (Butt, Russell, and Grigg 2004, 27). A stationary deep depression sitting over the ocean can fuel days of large swell.

Oceanographers identify two basic mechanisms in the production of waves: wind and gravity. Wind "pushes down" on the water; as the pressure is released, the depression springs up, under the force of surface tension, while the lump around the depression drops down. The result is random capillary waves (Butt, Russell, and Grigg 2004, 33). Capillary waves ruffle the ocean, which, in turn, "modifies" the air above, producing "turbulent eddies." These eddies become part of the wave structure, following the wave, increasing pressure over the troughs, decreasing the pressure over the crests, and further increasing the size of the eddies and the waves (Butt, Russell, and Grigg 2004, 34). In other words, by "roughening" the ocean surface, capillary waves enable the wind to get a better purchase; the waves increase in size, which gives the wind even more purchase and causes the waves to grow more quickly. At some point, capillary waves transform into gravity waves when gravity exceeds surface tension as the dominant restoring force (Butt, Russell, and Grigg 2004, 34–35). Gravity waves grow as a result of differences in pressure exerted

Storm waves, North Pacific, winter 1989. *Source:* National Oceanic and Atmospheric Administration, National Weather Service Collection.

on the rear (driven or upwind) slope and the front (advancing or down-wind) slope (Bird 2000, 7), although gravity also limits the size of waves (Butt, Russell, and Grigg 2004, 34–35).

While winds blowing across oceans form the overwhelming majority of waves, earthquakes and/or landslides can also produce waves—massive waves—called tsunamis. There is much debate among oceanographers as to whether surfers can ride tsunamis. Felipe Pomar, who won the world championship in 1965, believes he rode a tsunami in 1974 at La Isla (Peru). Pomar was on the beach when a strong earthquake struck for what he said felt like an eternity. After the ground ceased shaking, Pomar proceeded into the water for his surf. Around 15 minutes into the session, a strong current, "ten times as strong as anything I'd experienced at Sunset Beach," suddenly arose and began dragging Pomar out to sea. Within minutes he was a mile from shore in an ocean with "gigantic boils and whirlpools coming up out of the depths." Observing huge waves breaking perhaps a mile away to his left, Pomar "paddle[d] across the current, hoping to connect with the breaking waves before being swept to oblivion or swallowed by a tsunami." At the lineup, Pomar caught

a nice lefthander, climbing and dropping on the face. Part of me was screaming. "I must be mad! If I lose my board I'll be swept away and lost at sea!" But the other part was saying, "keep standing and turning. It's got good shape." The wave filled in, and I finally lost it, still a quarter mile from shore. As I paddled toward the beach what I saw shocked me. The wave I'd been riding kept going, then jacked up a fishing boat and threw it above a retaining wall and into a building, smashing it to bits. But if there had been 1,000 hungry lions on the sand I still would've gone in. I paddled around the debris and made it to shore. (Hynd 1989, 94)

Jose Borrero (2009), a surfer and research oceanographer with ASR (a New Zealand–based consultancy, which among other things advocates the use of submerged reefs for coastal protection and recreational enhancement), and associate of the Tsunami Research Center (University of Southern California), doubts Pomar rode a real tsunami and proposes that it was more likely a "shorter period artifact," the product of a tsunami "reflecting and scattering off underwater features." Comparing films of the Indian Ocean tsunami of December 26, 2004, Borrero (2009) notes that footage "from Sumatra shows…the near shore…flooded by…a bore front breaking over dry land" while footage from Thailand, where the shallower

> ## the indian ocean tsunami, december 26, 2004
> When the seabed is displaced by volcanic activity and earthquakes, it pushes surface water up until it is forced down by gravity. This movement of water causes a wave called a tsunami (Japanese for "harbor wave"). An earthquake at the interface of the India and Burma tectonic plates, 250 kilometers (about 150 mi.) south-southeast of Banda Aceh, Northern Sumatra, generated the Indian Ocean tsunami in 2004. In this case the quake uplifted the seabed several meters (1 m = 3.28 ft.) in a sudden, single jolt (Butt 2009, 154–56).

ocean floor would have broken up the tsunami, "shows something a bit more 'surf like;' one video even shows a huge plunging-type breaker at a beach resort [which appears] rideable."

After they form, waves radiate away from the source (e.g., wind depression, earthquake) in ever-widening circles, just as ripples travel away from the point of impact of a stone thrown into a pond. At the center of a storm, winds produce waves of varying lengths, sizes, and shapes. As they move away from the depression, waves become more regular, changing into low, broad, rounded swells. A sorting process also occurs as the longer, faster swells race to front, and the shorter, slower ones drop back. Typically organized as sets, swells can comprise anything from two to ten waves; in between the sets the ocean may be smooth or support smaller waves (Butt, Russell, and Grigg 2004, 43 and 45). Oceanographers, however, have yet to explain differences in swell composition (e.g., sets varying between 3 and 10 waves) and timing (e.g., sets spaced between 5 and 20 minutes apart, or "normal" sets interspersed with "super" sets) (Butt, Russell, and Grigg 2004, 47). While waves lose about 20 percent of their energy each day as they move through the ocean, they can still travel vast distances:

Storms in the Southern Ocean initiate the south-westerly swell that travels thousands of kilometres to arrive on the western . . . and southern shores of Australia, New Zealand, the Americas and Africa. South-westerly swell generated by gales south of Africa is transmitted across the Indian Ocean to the southern coasts of India and Sri Lanka and the western coast of Thailand. It reaches the southern coasts of Sumatra and Java, and other Indonesian islands as far east

as Timor. South-westerly swell originating south of Australia and New
Zealand moves across the Pacific Ocean to coasts between Chile,
California and Alaska, and the stormy waters south of South America
produce south-westerly swell across the Atlantic Ocean to West Africa and Western Europe (Portugal to the Hebrides). (Bird 2000, 8)

Waves cover similar distances in the northern hemisphere:

A north-westerly swell from the North Pacific arrives on the shores
between British Columbia, California and Central America. In the
North Atlantic a north-westerly swell extends to the coasts of Western Europe (Ireland to Portugal) and West Africa (Morocco to Sen-
egal). (Bird 2000, 8–9)

As these predominant swells move across the oceans they fan out and generate weaker tributaries. In the southern hemisphere, strong southwesterly
swells in the Southern Ocean (the seas around Antarctica) can produce
smaller southeasterly swells that arrive on the southeast coast of Australia (between Tasmania and Fraser Island), the east coast of New Zealand,
the Argentinean/Brazilian coast, and the southeast coast of Africa. In the
northern hemisphere, strong northwesterly swells in the North Pacific di-
verge with northeasterly swells arriving on the east coast of Asia, including Japan, China, and the Philippines, and extending south to the north
coast of New Guinea. In the North Atlantic the northwest swell also di-
verges into a northeast swell that reaches the east coasts of the Americas
from Cape Hatteras to the northeast coast of Brazil (Bird 2000, 8–9).

   The basic characteristic of a wave, and essential to its understanding,
is its period—that is, the time, measured in seconds, between successive
crests. Longer periods generally mean larger waves. Waves with periods
of less than 12 seconds are commonly referred to as windswell, while
those with periods over 12 seconds are typically described as groundswell.
Swells travel at approximately 1.5 times the period. Hence, a wave with
a 12-second period moves at about 18 knots (about 21 mph) and a wave
with an 18-second period moves at 27 knots (about 31 mph) ("Surf Forecasting" undated).

   Most of the energy in groundswell waves resides under the surface. In
the extract from *The Cruise of the Snark* that opens this chapter Jack London is only partially correct when he asserts that the water in the body of a
wave remains still. The water moves in a circular or orbital path, although
it does return to approximately where it began after a wave passes through.

Waves in longer period swells are not particularly steep, a condition that protects them to some degree from the decaying effects of wind ("Surf Forecasting" undated).

The transformation to surfable wave begins as the swell approaches the shoreline and the water depth decreases to the point where the ocean floor is about half the wave length (i.e., distance between successive crests). At this point the energy—the orbital motion—in the wave comes into contact with the ocean floor, and the friction slows or shoals the wave. The orbits of the water particles get smaller and eventually diminish to nothing at a depth equal to about half the wave length (Butt, Russell, and Grigg 2004, 41). Swells with periods of 10 seconds make contact with the ocean floor at 256 feet; 12 seconds at 369 feet; 14 seconds at 502 feet; 15 seconds at 576 feet; 18 seconds at 829 feet ("Surf Forecasting" undated) Professor Tony Dalrymple at the Center for Applied Coastal Research, University of Delaware, offers a wave calculator for estimating wave parameters (http://www.coastal.udel.edu/faculty/rad/wavetheory.html).

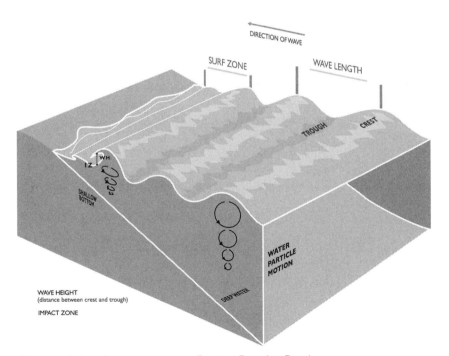

Characteristics of an ocean wave. *Source:* Douglas Booth.

Shoaling alters the shape of the orbiting particles of the wave, squashing the circular orbits into ellipses (Butt, Russell, and Grigg 2004, 41) and effectively pushing the energy in the base of the swell upward; this causes the crest to increase in height and sharpen its shape. The take-off zone, where the wave begins to break, occurs where the depth of the water is around 1.3 times the height of the wave (i.e., a 4-foot wave breaks in just over 5 feet of water; a 6-foot wave breaks in nearly 8 feet of water; a 10-foot wave will break in about 13 feet, and a 15-footer breaks in around 19 feet of water) ("Surf Forecasting" undated; Butt, Russell, and Grigg 2004, 61–62).

Variations, however, are enormous. At Pipeline 10-foot waves break in less than 3 feet of water. The primary determinant of the depth at which a wave breaks, and its form as surf, is the bathymetry—seabed topography—and particularly the suddenness with which it changes (Butt, Russell, and Grigg 2004, 62). A gently sloping bathymetry means that the crest of the wave travels only a little faster than the bottom; these waves typically have less power, and they crumble (Butt, Russell, and Grigg 2004, 63). By contrast,

> if the transition from deep to shallow is very sudden...then, momentarily, the wave is inevitably [in] very shallow water without having broken. At this point, the height of the wave is quite significant compared with the depth of water, and the distance between the top of the wave and the sea floor is much more than the bottom of the wave and the sea floor. [Thus] the speed of the top of the wave will be greater than the bottom of the wave. This will cause the wave to throw out as it breaks, making it steep, hollow and fast. (Butt, Russell, and Grigg 2004, 62)

All the big-wave breaks feature a radical variation in the marine contour, from deep to shallow. At Jaws (Maui), for example, the water jumps from a trench over 100 feet deep to a reef of just 20 feet. Sharp variations magnify the wave energy over shallow water.

Variations in bathymetry mean that breaking waves assume countless forms as they release their energy. But the basic categories are *spilling breaker, plunging breaker,* and *surging breaker.* While the front of a spilling breaker is not much higher than the back, the profile of a plunging breaker undergoes radical transformation as it moves into shallow water; sometimes the front of the wave "sucks out" below sea level. In some extreme cases such as Teahupo'o (Tahiti), the front of the wave can measure 10 times the height of the back (Butt, Russell, and Grigg 2004, 64–65).

A sudden change in bathymetry can magnify wave energy and radically modify the form of a wave. Dale Hunter, The Island (New Zealand), 2005. *Source:* Mark Stevenson.

As well as causing waves to slow down and break, the bathymetry also causes waves to change direction (refract), and to wrap into point breaks or bend around reefs. Refractions are either concave or convex. Concave refraction occurs when the wave bends inward. For example, a straight line of swell approaching a shallow reef or sandbar with deeper water on either side will slow down over the underwater feature but maintain its speed in the deeper water. As a result the swell will "bend in from both sides, towards the shallower water" and effectively "concentrate all the energy" on the reef or sandbar; the concentrated, or focused, energy forms a "peak" (Butt, Russell, and Grigg 2004, 52). Reefs or slabs of rock sited in open water and bounded by relatively deeper water on either side (e.g., Cortes Bank off San Diego; Cyclops, Western Australia) can push the waves up to three to five times as high as in deep water (*Making the Call* 2003, ch. 4 and ch. 5). Such convergences of energy produce "bowl-type" waves that can break with inordinate power.

Convex refraction causes the wave to bend outward "away from the deep water" in a process known as "defocusing" (Butt, Russell, and Grigg 2004, 52–53). For example, when a line of swell approaches a headland or point with a reef running parallel to the headland / point outside of which is the deeper water of the bay, it slows and refracts, perhaps to around 90 degrees of the line of approach, while that remaining in the deeper water maintains its speed as it continues to travel toward the shoreline. Although defocusing at point breaks tends to reduce the power and size of waves, the wall—surfable face—can be quite long, and in some cases (e.g., Jeffreys Bay [South Africa], Kirra [Queensland, Australia], Tavarua [Fiji], Ala Moana [O'ahu], Shipstern Bluff [Tasmania]) the wave increases in size after take-off (Butt, Russell, and Grigg 2004, 53). Long period swell is a critical ingredient for good surf at point breaks. In a groundswell, waves "bend around the point" and "hook in and reel-off down the line," while in windswell waves often "go 'fat' into the middle of the bay" or "crumble [in] sections" (Butt, Russell, and Grigg 2004, 57).

Wind helps shape the form of a breaking wave. Offshore winds blowing directly onto the wall of a wave will groom its face and even hold up a falling lip or crumbling section. Of course, strong offshore winds may hinder a surfer paddling-in to the wave and dropping down the face. Wind was a factor in Jay Moriarty's "wipeout for the millennium," as *Surfer* called his fall on the 20-foot wave at Maverick's in 1994. Wind coming up the face of the wave drove spray into Moriarty's face as he rose to his feet; the strength of the wind was such that it caught underneath the surfboard and tossed it over Moriarty's head and the crest (Warshaw 2000, 2).

Climatologists have identified a series of cycles in the movement of the atmosphere and oceans, including the North Pacific Oscillation, the Arctic Oscillation, the Antarctic Oscillation, and the *El Niño* Southern Oscillation (Butt 2009). Capitalizing on increased computer power and advanced computer modeling, oceanographers are now describing variations in atmospheric pressure, storms in different oceans, and swell size over extended periods in the past (Butt 2009). The notion of swell cycles appears credible in the light of the swells of 1939, 1953, 1969, 1983, and 2001, which have acquired legendary status in surfing folklore.

Four large swells lashed California in 1939. On May 17, surfing pioneer Wally Froiseth reported that "large" waves quickly grew "big," then "huge" and then "monstrous." Four months later, in the last week of September, another swell hit Southern California from the south, washing out many coastal roads; at Malibu surfers rode 15-foot waves before strong winds and heavy rain forced them from the water. On Thanksgiving Day a huge swell hit California from the west and on New Year's Eve another produced 20-foot waves that, according to surf photographer Leroy Grannis, broke beyond the end of Hermosa Beach Pier (Warshaw 2004, 618).

In January 1953 a large westerly swell hit California over a period of days, forcing the evacuation of many houses along the coast. At Rincon, south of Santa Barbara, a terrified Ricky Grigg (1998, 29) rode his first "triple-overhead wave," which ended up pounding him and rolling him underwater. At Santa Monica, two surfers rode 12- to 14-foot waves that broke well beyond the end of the pier (Wolf 2000, 30).

The swell that generated 50-foot waves in Hawai'i and 20-foot waves in Southern California in the first week of December 1969 is often referred to as the biggest of the 20th century and the biggest of surfing's first "Golden Age" (Duane 1998b). The swell emanated from three overlapping storms in the North Pacific:

> The first was identified on November 27, off the Kamchatka Peninsula. On the 28th, the fast-growing east-moving storm met with another low pressure area and doubled in size, and by the following day 60 mile per hour winds were blowing across a front measuring 2,000 miles, from just north of Hawaii to the Aleutian Islands. Furthermore, the storm remained nearly stationary for more than 24 hours, helping to generate even bigger swells. Meanwhile, a third storm, smaller but still powerful, began tracking along the initial storm's wake. (Warshaw 2004, 619)

The first waves reached Hawai'i in the afternoon of December 1 and turned the North Shore of O'ahu into "a morass of six-story storm surf" (*Riding Giants* 2004, ch. 10). On the morning of December 4, a small group of surfers including Wally Froiseth, Fred Hemmings, Jim Blears, Randy Rarick, and Rolf Aurness rode 20-foot waves at Makaha and in the afternoon Greg Noll took off on a 35-footer (see chapter 5) which many cite as the largest wave ridden in the 20th century to that point (Warshaw 2004, 619–20). The large swell reached Southern California the same day and lasted until December 8. Ricky Grigg was there, and at La Jolla Cove (San Diego) he rode a 20-footer for ½ mile (Grigg 1998, 33).

In 1983 a series of storms over two months between mid-January and mid-March produced almost continuous overhead waves in California, while big-wave surfers enjoyed almost three weeks of rideable waves in Hawai'i at Waimea Bay (Warshaw 2004, 620). The swell of 1983, says surfing historian Matt Warshaw (2004, 620), contributed to the reemergence of big-wave riding:

After years of concentrating on professional surf contests and zippy small-wave performance surfing, the surf media, for the first time since the late '60s, began to refocus on big-wave riding. *Surfer* ran a Waimea photograph on the cover of the July 1983 issue (the first Waimea shot so used since 1965), and published two articles "Whatever Happened to Big-Wave Riding?" and "Dinner at Charlie's," both loaded with 1983 Waimea photos.

In early July 2001 a gale 1,000 miles off the east coast of Australia between New Zealand and New Caledonia generated three days of double-overhead waves along the east coast of Australia. A light offshore breeze accompanied the swell and, combined with sunny skies, made conditions especially favorable. Four-time world champion surfer Mark Richards even postulated that "this could be as good as it's ever going to get" (Warshaw 2004, 621).

Although the swell that hit O'ahu on January 28, 1998, has not won the same legendary status as those discussed above, it did produce an 80-foot colossus at Outside Log Cabins, into which Dan Moore towed Ken Bradshaw. Describing the moment, Bradshaw recalled:

> We'd been tracking a few waves, getting used to the field. So when this thing came in, I knew it was a big wave. And it just kept building and building. It was absolutely enormous. I knew it was going to be the biggest wave I'd ever had. I'm going, "this thing's amazing how big it is." It was just so much bigger than anything I'd ever ridden. I motioned to Dan…, grabbed the rope, and we pull out. So we get out to the channel. [Dan] just stops the machine and he goes [into this hyper-excited pitch]: "That was it man, you should have seen that; that was the most radical thing I've ever seen. That wave must have been 80 feet; it could have been 100 feet. That was radical." (*Extreme Surfing* 2000, ch. 5)

The waters off Durban, South Africa, are reputed to consistently produce enormous, although not necessarily surfable, waves. Here the Agulhas Current, which travels from northeast to southwest, meets swells moving southwest to northeast (Casey 2010, ch. 12). The current pumps energy into the swells, causing them to become steeper and higher. The generally accepted biggest wave ever sighted was in the North Pacific; it measured 109 feet (Butt, Russell, and Grigg 2004, 79). Surfline, a prominent surf forecasting service (www.surfline.com), calculates that Cortes Bank could produce rideable wave faces of 150 feet based on a 30-foot swell hitting the reef and being magnified five times (*Making the Call* 2003, ch. 7).

> **megatsunami**   Geological history reveals that volcanic ocean islands have sometimes collapsed. Such collapses may displace hundreds of cubic kilometers (1 km = 0.62 mi.) of rock into the sea and produce "splashes" of unimaginable proportions, generating waves that scientists call megatsunamis. In 2001 Steven Ward (a geophysicist at University of California–Santa Cruz) and Simon Day (a geologist at University College, London) identified the Cumbre Vieja volcano on La Palma in the Canary Islands as a candidate to collapse. Such an event, they hypothesized, could generate a megatsunami that would destroy most of the Canary Islands before making its way across the Atlantic Ocean to the east coast of North America, where it "would obliterate everything up to 20 km [about 12 mi.] inland" (Butt 2009, 166–67).

How much power does a breaking wave release? While power varies between breaks and depends on local conditions, *Storm Surfers* (2007, ch. 5) calculates that a 20-meter-wide (65-ft.) section of lip falling at 70 kilometers per hour (45 mph) on a 10-meter (30-ft.) wave traveling toward shore at 30 kilometers per hour (20 mph) would produce around 500,000 kilograms (550 tons) of water moving at over 100 kilometers per hour (60 mph) (conversions are approximate). Using an accelerometer, *Storm Surfers* (2007, ch. 6) measured the g-forces on a model of a human body thrown into the whitewater of a 20-footer. It recorded two 10.5 g-force impacts and four other significant impacts in the space of three seconds—powerful enough to snap surfboards and crack femurs, spines, and necks (Moses 1982, 88).

Among aficionados, however, the pleasures not only outweigh the risks, they fuel a fanatical obsession. While sociologists explain this obsession in terms of social relationships and peer pressure, biologists search for answers in pleasure-inducing neurochemicals.

biological science

Refrains of pleasure saturate surfing literature. In one of the first European records of riding waves, Captain James Cook described in his journal a "most supreme pleasure" experienced by a Tahitian who, by catching waves in his canoe, was "driven on so fast and so smoothly by the sea" (Marcus 2008, 8). Gidget, Frederick Kohner's fictional teenage character whose exploits on the beach and in the water at Malibu helped popularize surfing in the late 1950s, described the sensation of "shooting the curl" as "out of this world.... It positively surpasses every living emotion I've ever had" (*Riding Giants* 2004, ch. 9). The pleasure may be tantalizingly brief, "just one turn," but that's "all it takes," says Gerry Lopez, to "keep pulling you back—to have another moment—it never ends" (*Step into Liquid* 2004, ch. 1).

What are the sources of these pleasures? As Cook, Gidget, and Lopez intimate, much of the pleasure of surfing derives from the speed of driving across the wall of a wave and the associated feeling of balancing on a moving board. Philosopher and sociologist Roger Caillois (1958/2001) called these feelings—which he associated with a number of physical activities including swinging, waltzing, skiing, mountain climbing, and tightrope walking—*ilinx,* or vertigo. In surfing, the take-off, the drop down the face of the wall, and the first driving turn off the bottom engage feelings of *ilinx.* Big waves accentuate these feelings (Farmer 1992).

Laurie Towner recalls with crystal clarity the feelings of *ilinx* he experienced on a big wave at Shipstern Bluff (Tasmania), one that earned him a cover of the Australian surf magazine *Tracks* ("The Surfer's Bible"):

> I was just in the perfect spot and...I knew that if I just took off and made it, it was going to be the best feeling I've ever had. I remember...I got down [a little step] and did my bottom turn [and] I looked up and saw the thickest piece of water just throw over me and it was like this huge green barrel about twenty times bigger than anything I had ever stood in before. I got spat out and had the craziest adrenaline rushing through me. (Webber 2009, 48)

Mark Richards describes the feeling of "conquering one drop" at Waimea Bay as "better than anything" (Cralle 2001, 311). Professional surfer Pat O'Connell calls the drop at Teahupo'o unsurpassable pleasure:

> When you do get to your feet, that sliding down the face, you just can't recreate that anywhere. The feeling of...weightless, your fins are above your head and you're pushing down to really get down the face. There is a moment where your board is not grabbing on anything. If you are lucky your fins grab and you come through that section. (*Blackwater* 2005, ch. 6)

Most of the pleasure in surfing—what aficionados call "stoke" (or "hopupu" in Hawai'ian) "a fully embodied feeling of satisfaction, joy and pride"

(Evers 2006, 230–31; see also Poirier 2003)—is undoubtedly tied to *ilinx*. *Storm Surfers* (2007, ch. 6) quantifies aspects of speed and balance associated with towing-in to a 20-foot wave:

> At the moment of releasing the rope, [the surfer] briefly slows down from 38 kilometers an hour to 30 kilometers an hour, but then experiences a massive acceleration [down the face of the wave and through the bottom turn] from 30 kilometers an hour to 66 kilometers an hour in just 6 seconds. In everyday terms, this is similar to standing on top of a bus and turning a corner at 60 kilometers an hour with nothing to hold on to.

However, other aspects of surfing, including "dealing with forces of nature" and the "mental and physical challenges" they pose (Thomas 2008), performing in front of peers for prestige, and social relationships, also physically envelop surfers' bodies.

Big-wave legend Brock Little (1989, 113) captures well the affects of extreme surf: "So much adrenaline pumps through that sometimes I have to yell or shake my arms, legs, and head to try and off-load the jitters." Pride undoubtedly motivates surfers to deal with their fears in order to earn the plaudits of peers. Recounting the moment of the take-off on his

Accelerating into stoke: Ross Clarke-Jones turning off the bottom at Papatowai, 2002. *Source:* Mark Stevenson.

cover-shot ride at Shipstern Bluff, Laurie Towner described the pressure he felt in the mere presence of former world champion Andy Irons, who was in the water nearby at the time (*Tracks* June 2006, second cover). In this flickering moment, Towner brushed aside the affect of fear, which, like pride, is also embodied. "The shame one feels in failing to meet the requirements of certain waves," Clif Evers (2004, 36) argues, "must itself be hidden as an ugly scar is hidden, lest it offends the one who looks." Of course, shame can never really be hidden. "I've lost a couple of friends," says Laird Hamilton, "who I thought were great watermen but who didn't come for me during a crisis in the impact zone. I won't ever look at 'em the same. And they know that. Not a thing they can do about it. It's like a brand (makes a sizzling noise). And there won't be another chance" (Jenkins 1997, 116).

Friendships can contribute another strong affective element to surfing. Whether searching for waves on surfari or partaking in a surfing session, discovering good waves with friends is, Clif Evers reminds us, a moving experience. Once, after trekking through thick, bug-infested jungle, Evers and his friends discovered a bay with perfect wrapping surf. Evers remembers one friend who "looked me in the eye and with the utmost intimacy said, 'We did it.' A shiver ran down my spine" (Evers 2004, 36). Such sensations (and those of *ilinx*) are "how [our] bodies feel and what motivate us": they "establish our relations to objects, initiate interest in certain movements, and amplify our experiences so that we learn" (Evers 2006, 230 and 235). Importantly, Evers's conceptualization of these sensations, or affects, weaves together social and biological factors, which scientists conventionally keep apart but which the preceding examples and comments suggest are interdependent. In other words, the biological and

---

shaming   Sometimes surfers publicly shame their peers as a political strategy to reinforce their social dominance at a particular break. Koby Abberton directed a torrent of abuse at Nick Nass during a tow-in session when the latter shied away from a "contorting barrel" breaking "feet from a dry ledge": "I'm never towing you into another wave for as long as I live. The closest you're ever gunna get to my ski again is when I run over you" (Griggs 2003, 81).

sociocultural characteristics of extreme surfers, as a subset of sensation seekers, interact and reinforce each other.

Research into the biology of sensation seeking identifies the key components as genes, neurotransmitters, hormones, and the orienting reflex—that is, the way in which an individual responds to a novel stimulus (e.g., Zuckerman 1979 and 1994). Zuckerman (1994, 385) attributes around 50 percent of sensation-seeking behavior to genes; some studies suggest an association between the D4 dopamine receptor (D4DR) exon III—the specific gene that controls the use of dopamine in the brain—and novelty seeking (e.g., Sheese et al. 2007, 1039; Zuckerman and Kuhlman 2000, 1016). Zuckerman (1994, 381) proposes that individuals will respond to stimuli in ways that reflect their genetic makeup. For example, parents who are very much sensation seekers themselves (high sensation seekers) are more "likely to encourage sensation-seeking exploration in their children" than parents who are low sensation seekers, who "may be frightened by potential risks and attempt to discourage sensation seeking" in their offspring (Zuckerman 1984, 382). But the degree of parental influence ultimately depends on the child's genetic disposition (Zuckerman 1994, 382).

At the biological level, scientists single out monoamine neurotransmitters (dopamine, norepinephrine, serotonin) and gonadal hormones (hormones produced by the testes and ovaries—e.g., testosterone) as the basic drivers of sensation seeking (e.g., Zuckerman 1994; Kotler 2006). Dopamine is the key neurotransmitter. It is "the substance of the 'life instinct'. Its absence results in a 'living death,' sans activity, sans desire, sans interest, sans joy, sans sensation seeking," while "overactivity...can produce an unrelenting and eventually exhausting mania" (Zuckerman 1994, 387). The biographies of many extreme surfers reveal a hyperactivity suggestive of abundant dopamine. In different parts of the brain, dopamine serves different functions. It may "energize active exploration of the social and physical environment" or "provide the positive arousal and reward associated with novel and intense stimulation" (Zuckerman 1994, 385). Some neurophysiologists propose that chronic elevation of dopamine reduces the availability of dopamine receptors, which in turn limits their ability to respond to chemical signaling. Dulling the responsiveness of the brain's reward pathways may produce desensitization to a stimulus whereby the individual requires more dopamine to maintain the same physiological response. These findings help explain apparent addictions to physical activity and why some surfers constantly seek bigger, faster, steeper, longer waves, just as drug addicts seek more frequent and higher doses (Franken, Zijlstra, and Muris 2006, 299; Esch and Stefano 2004, 242).

In addition to dopamine, two other neurotransmitters are critical to understanding the biology of sensation seeking: norepinephrine and serotonin. Norepinephrine "provides the arousal associated with novel and intense stimuli and amplifies the reaction to such stimuli. It also accounts for the enhanced capacity for focused attention" (Zuckerman 1994, 386), critical, for example, to taking-off on huge waves. Serotonin "inhibits behavior in the presence of novel or potentially threatening stimuli. Its behavioral function is…immobility or indecisiveness" (Zuckerman 1994, 386), which is a detrimental trait in extreme surf. It is reasonable to assume that extreme surfers have higher levels of norepinephrine and lower levels of serotonin than the average population.

Referring to hormones, Zuckerman (1994, 386) links testosterone to a range of personality traits including "sensation seeking, impulsivity, social dominance, and sociability." High sensation seekers demonstrate a stronger orienting reflex compared with low sensation seekers. However, the response of high sensation seekers to subsequent presentations of a stimulus is weaker and "no greater than that of low sensation seekers, unless the stimulus is of some special significance or interest" (Zuckerman 1994, 374–75; see also Esch and Stefano 2004, 242). Again, this may help explain why some surfers constantly travel in search of new waves.

In the end, we know very little about the neurobiology and psychophysiology of pleasure induced by movement (Kotler 2006), in part because of the difficulties in assessing neurochemical reactions in the human body during physical activity, particularly activity outside the laboratory. Recent work suggests any number of substances and pathways in the central nervous system—many of which probably overlap—can produce pleasurable sensations (Esch and Stefano 2004, 236; Ventura, Morrone, and Puglisi-Allegra 2007).

The interface between the biological and the social body is currently little understood (Ford and Brown 2006, 120). The underrepresentation of women in 20th century physical activities, including surfing (Booth 2001b), is a good example. Buzzy Trent may have rejoiced at the sight of the "beautiful, well-shaped girl riding a 6-foot wave with the wind blowing through her hair," but he objected to "girls riding (or attempting to ride) big waves": they are too "emotional," "tend to panic," and because they are "weaker than men" they are less likely to survive heavy wipeouts (Warshaw 2000, 109). Such views effectively reduced women to "props" in the big-wave culture of O'ahu in the 1950s and '60s. According to Fred van Dyke,

> You took the best looking woman you could find, sat her on the beach so she could watch everything you did, then you went out and bragged to your friends about her. So she'd sit on the beach all day, get sunburned and dehydrated, and the guy would come in and get pissed off because she didn't see his best ride. That was the scene. It was machismo to the nth degree. (Warshaw 1997, 111)

But how much influence does testosterone have on an individual's engagement, and disengagement, with different types and styles of physical activity?

Women regularly venture into big surf; indeed their mention in Hawai-'ian legends (see chapter 2) suggests they were inextricably involved in the development of the sport. Among the better-known contemporary female extreme surfers are Linda Benson, Maya Gabeira, Joyce Hoffman, Betty Depolito, Maria Souza, Layne Beachley, Sarah Gerhardt, Andrea Moller, Jamilah Star, Keala Kennelly, Kim Hamrock, and Jennie Useldinger. Souza surfed Jaws with her then-husband Laird Hamilton before teaming up with Andrea Moller to tow-in at the same break in 2006 (Chase 2008, 138). Gerhardt is known as the first woman to ride Maverick's, while Gabeira, four-time winner of the XXL Women's Best Performance award, has surfed Maverick's, Waimea, Todos Santos, Teahupo'o, and Dungeons (South Africa). On August 11, 2009, Gabeira rode what some believe is the biggest wave ever surfed by a woman, a 25-foot monster at Dungeons ("Dungeons Delivers" 2009).

Zuckerman (1994, 377) notes that "prenatal gonadal hormones affect the developing brain of the fetus" and that

> girls exposed to excessive testosterone during the fetal period exhibit more typically masculine patterns of play after birth. Compared with girls of their own age and their own female siblings, they tend to prefer "rough-and-tumble" play to "dolls" and "house." Similar gender reversed play effects have been found in boys exposed to estrogen during the prenatal period.

Looking closer at the relationship between hormones and sensation seeking, Jon Rosenblitt and his colleagues (2001) identify a strong correlation between cortisol—a hormone released in response to stress—and high sensation seeking in women.

Hormonal difference *within* the sexes may explain some of the positions in the debates over staging competitions in extreme surf. Holding competitions at Teahupo'o, which has assumed the mantle of the world's most dangerous wave (see chapter 4), fuels debate among professional surfers. Seven-time women's world champion Layne Beachley admits there are "mixed emotions" about women surfing Teahupo'o: "Some girls hate it, some girls love it, and some girls love to hate it" (*Blackwater* 2005, ch. 12). Beachley is a staunch advocate for the contest:

> Women's surfing needs Teahupo'o. It gives us...credibility and respect....The guys show us more respect and the world takes notice when we charge out there. It is a fantastic opportunity to promote women's surfing and to put us on the world stage. (*Blackwater* 2005, ch. 12)

Four-time world champion Lisa Anderson believes that women need to spend "more time in the water at Teahupo'o to 'figure' it out." But she also concedes the dangers. During one contest Anderson was caught inside and almost drowned before being pulled out by the rescue crew: "That was my goodbye—see ya, I'm not coming back" (*Blackwater* 2005, ch. 12).

Keala Kennelly scorns suggestions that Teahupo'o is no place for women. The break is "dangerous for anyone who does not have the skills or drive to challenge themselves by attempting to ride it," she says, adding that "what you are carting around between your legs is of no significance" (Chase 2008, 148). Professional surfer Neco Padaratz probably agrees. After he wiped out on a six-foot wave in one contest, the Brazilian was pushed by the current into the impact zone where walls of white water repeatedly slammed him into the coral reef. At one point his leg rope caught on coral and "tied" him to the reef. "I was only saved," he said, "because I was wearing a green helmet which the rescue team on Jet Skis could see against the white water." Contest director Chris O'Callaghan remembers a dazed Padaratz on the Jet Ski: "His eyes were going to the back of his head. He was white. He came through, and then went into shock mode. It was a really tough situation." "The helmet saved my life," Padaratz said, and "I had cuts all over my body. It was the worst pain in my life. I don't deserve this for [first prize, $30,000]. I have so much more in my life. I want my kid to know his father" (*Blackwater* 2005, ch. 12).

Of course, many of the embodied feelings and affects of surfing are gender neutral; they have no "meaning beyond sensations and movement"

Gender disappears inside the barrel. Jamie Gordon, The Island (New Zealand), 2005. *Source:* Mark Stevenson.

(Ford and Brown 2006, 163). Indeed, gender typically disappears under mountains of collapsing water or deep inside cylindrical waves. In these conditions, it's impossible to tell the sexes apart.

Science offers more complete explanations for what many surfers know and have learned about the ocean and waves through experience. Moreover, as I shall show in chapter 7, science will undoubtedly contribute significantly to the sport in the future, particularly in the area of predicting swells and directing surfers to the best waves breaking in the world at any time. On the other hand, science has proved less adept at explaining the obsessive pleasures of surfing (Kotler 2006). One of the problems for science in trying to explain pleasure lies in the challenge of integrating biological and cultural factors into a single coherent account. As of now, much remains to be done. It appears surfers will continue to have a better understanding than scientists of the lure of oceanic energy, at least for the foreseeable future.

4. breaks

The grass grows right down to the water at Waikiki Beach, and within fifty feet of the everlasting sea. The trees also grow down to the salty edge of things, and one sits in their shade and looks seaward at a majestic surf thundering in on the beach to one's very feet. Half a mile out, where is the reef, the white-headed combers thrust suddenly skyward out of the placid turquoise-blue and come rolling in to shore. One after another they come, a mile long, with smoking crests, the white battalions of the infinite army of the sea. And one sits and listens to the perpetual roar, and watches the unending procession, and feels tiny and fragile before this tremendous force expressing itself in fury and foam and sound. Indeed, one feels microscopically small.

Jack London (1911, 67)

in his description of Waikiki Beach in the early 20th century, Jack London graphically captures the lure of big surf and its sheer unbridled power. The thundering, ocean-splitting, earth-vibrating, and captivating suspense of big surf not only reveals the raw forces of Mother Nature, it exposes the ultimate insignificance and powerlessness of the human species. In this chapter I examine the oceanographic features of "a short dozen" (i.e., 11) breaks that produce extreme waves: Cortes Bank, Cyclops, Dungeons, Jaws, Maverick's, Outside Log Cabins, Pipeline, Shipstern Bluff, Teahupo'o, Todos Santos, and Waimea. Surfers are never more than temporary guests at these locations. In chapter 5, I discuss the surfers who have earned legendary status riding these breaks. But irrespective of their heroism and death-defying achievements on individual waves, they know they can never claim to have conquered Mother Nature; one mistake or miscalculation on almost any wave at these extreme breaks may end it all.

cortes bank (off san diego)

In the world of extreme surfing breaks, Cortes Bank, about 100 miles west of San Diego, is, according to Surfline, in "a league of its own." As noted in chapter 3, Surfline calculates that Cortes Bank could generate rideable wave faces of 150 feet. Mike Parsons won the Ride of the Year in the 2001 XXL Big Wave Awards on a 66-foot face at Cortes Bank (*Making the Call* 2003, ch. 7). With an even larger swell running, Parsons returned to Cortes Bank in January 2008 for another session after which he predicted that "it's only a matter of time" before someone scores a 100-foot wave there: "It's getting closer and closer now.... There were several big peaks that jumped up at the top of the reef outside of us that could not have been too far off that size. If you put yourself in the right place at the right time, it will happen" ("Biggest Cortes" 2008).

Cortes Bank is a 20-mile long underwater island rising from over a mile deep to just six feet below the surface. The island is a swell magnet. Swells from the west and northwest track along the entire length of the Bank to converge on a corner of reef where the energy concentrates and dramatically increases the height of waves into a classic peak. Conditions are fickle at Cortes Bank, which is typically exposed to swells from multiple directions and strong winds; the Bank records winds of 20 knots over 360 days a year. There are no landmarks or indicators to line up the take-off zone (*Making the Call* 2003, ch. 7), which big-wave rider and journalist Evan Slater describes as "a half-mile chunk of reef forever doomed to 360-degree confusion" (Warshaw 2004, 137).

Cortes Bank has been known as a shipping hazard for centuries. In the late 1960s California surfers Walter and Flippy Hoffman proposed that the Bank could be surfed. Early in 1990 surf photographer Larry "Flame" Moore flew to the site and photographed 30-foot waves from the air; later that year he returned to the Bank in a boat with three surfers who rode a few 8-foot waves. In January 2001 Moore coordinated Project Neptune, a one day excursion to Cortes Bank involving two boats, a plane, three personal watercraft (PWC), six cameramen and two tow-in teams (Mike Parsons and Brad Gerlach, and Ken "Skindog" Collins and Peter Mel). The trip was especially profitable for Parsons: his 66-foot wave of the year award won him $60,000 (Warshaw 2004, 137–38).

cyclops (western australia)

Originally named Greg's Knoll after a local abalone diver who discovered the break, Cyclops is a semi-secret wave that occasionally breaks on a barnacle-covered, knee-deep reef around an island a mile or so offshore near Esperance in the remote southwestern corner of Australia. Considered "borderline" rideable, descriptions of Cyclops invariably highlight the contorted shapes of the wave and the thundering noise of lips detonating on the reef. The waves "run out of water and turn inside out in a heartbeat, twisting into tormented shapes straight out of a horror movie. The speed with which the water moves up the face of the wave makes it incredibly hard to surf. . . . It's as close as you can go to unrideable" (Shorty 2005, 29). The "thunder of the lip hitting the reef [makes] the hair stand up on the back of your neck" (Shorty 2005, 26). "If the Devil was ever going surfing," muses surf photographer Andrew Buckley, "it'd be out here at Cyclops" (Doherty 2008, 69th moment).

Cyclops's notoriety as an extreme break followed a highly publicized surfari to the site in 2005 by the Abberton brothers (Sunny, Jai, and Koby), fellow Bra Boy Mark Matthews, and two local surfers: Mick "Beef" O'Keefe and Greg (*Bra Boys* 2006, ch. 14; Shorty 2005).

Contorted horror: Wave faces at many extreme surfing breaks contort into spectacular shapes that conjure sheer fear. Todd Robertson watches at The Island (New Zealand), 2000. *Source:* Mark Stevenson.

anatomy of an extreme surfer   In 1998 Koby Abberton won a World Qualifying Series contest in ferocious 12- to 15-foot waves at Teahupo'o (Tahiti). Over the following years, he gave standout performances at Jaws (Hawai'i) and Cloud-break (Fiji), earning him numerous cover shots on surfing magazines and a reputation as a leading extreme surfer. Pro-fessional surfer and winner of the Eddie Aikau memorial con-test Bruce Irons calls Abberton one of surfing's "biggest psycho charging pioneers" and "one of the heaviest guys in the world" (*Bra Boys* 2006, ch. 13).

The Abbertons arranged the surfari to Cyclops to celebrate the acquit-tal of Jai, who had been charged with the murder of a local Maroubra standover man during an altercation. (For the same incident, Koby was charged with being an accessory after the fact to murder, perverting the course of justice, and hindering a police investigation; he was acquitted of the accessory charge—which carried a prison term of up to 15 years— and was later found guilty of perverting the course of justice, for which he received a nine-month suspended sentence.) A recognized extreme surfer, Koby found Cyclops to be "the heaviest wave in Australia," and he can-didly admits that the break "scares" him (*Bra Boys* 2006, ch. 14). On this particular trip he wiped out and cut a vein, which required 18 stitches: "I knew I was going to [hit] the reef and I tried to put my hand out to [protect] my head" but "I felt a nick and severed [a] vein in my wrist" (Jones 2005). A photograph of Mark Matthews at Cyclops on this trip made the cover of *Tracks,* which proclaimed "Psyclops! Australia's Most Psychotic Wave" (*Tracks* October 2005).

dungeons (hout bay, cape town)

Another fickle wave in an unpredictable quarter of the South Atlan-tic Ocean, near Cape Town, South Africa, Dungeons breaks over sev-eral hundred meters (1 m = 3.28 ft.) of kelp beds and ledges. While some have questioned Dungeons' credentials as a big-wave location, Cheyne Horan, four-times world champion runner-up, and two-times runner-up in the XXL Big Wave awards, calls the break the "Waimea of Africa"; he considers it "a premier big-wave spot" with "big faces, long walls and heavy take-offs" (Horan undated). Grant Washburn, a local at Maverick's (see below), agrees; his description of a particularly brutal wipeout and hold down offers some insight into why surfers call the break Dungeons. After being "sucked over the falls and pinned to the bottom," Washburn felt "the weight of the wave...crushing the air out of me":

> I was still face down, planted on the bottom, and was getting a bit concerned that it would never let me go. I pushed up to my hands and knees, but it felt like an elephant was on my back. There was a momentary release of pressure, and I jumped like a frog into the foamy mayhem. (Masterton 2006a)

Pierre De Villiers and Peter Button surfed Dungeons in the early 1980s when it was known as The Sentinel, after the imposing granite outcrop overlooking the break. The following decade Cass Collier and Ian Armstrong began to surf Dungeons on a regular basis, hitching lifts to the break on fishing trawlers launched from the adjacent harbor at Hout Bay. In 1999 Collier and Armstrong won the first World Big Wave Team Championships at Todos Santos (Mexico) (see below) (Masterton 2006b, 2010).

Notwithstanding Dungeons' reputation for being erratic, surfing lore records some memorable sessions. In July 2006 Greg Long rode a 65-foot face at Dungeons to win the Biggest Wave in the XXL Awards; in July 2008, Long paddled-in to a 25-foot wave at Dungeons, which won him the Ride of the Year in the XXL Awards. Long captures the drama of the latter, which occurred during a heat of the Big Wave Africa competition:

> I paddled straight out...and right off the bat we all got cleaned up by a big 25-foot set. It just steamrolled me and...broke my board. I paddled back...and sure enough another set, just as big,...caught us all inside again. I was so far out it actually put me in perfect position for the wave. I just put my head down and paddled my heart out...just thinking I've got to catch a wave. The whole wall extended all the way to the channel. I remember taking off thinking, I'm going to get bulldozed on this one but I might as well at least try. I took a high line up into it...and...everything went into slow motion at that point. I've never been in a barrel quite that wide, especially paddling-in on a 9'8" [surfboard]. It's a real different feeling being inside of a barrel and trying to control the board. It had two sections throw at me. At one point I didn't think I was going to make it but the foam ball came up underneath and...actually gave me a little extra

projection forward. I just remember thinking, got to take the high line out.... I was able to sink low...and felt my feet dig into my board, just trying to hold an edge. That was it, yeah, probably one of the best rides of my life. ("Ride of the Year" 2009)

The following year at Dungeons, during a swell delivering sets in the 20 to 25 feet range, Maya Gabeira rode a wave that some surfers claim is the biggest ever ridden by a woman ("Dungeons Delivers" 2009).

jaws (maui)

A big-wave colossus on the north coast of Maui, Jaws was initially a favorite site for extreme windsurfers and attained the early name of Atom Blaster because "it broke like an atomic bomb" (Warshaw 2004, 302). According to Darrick Doerner, the name Jaws surfaced after a particularly big day at the break in which he towed Laird Hamilton into a wave that "made him look like an ant." "I was just shaking my head at what was right behind him," said Doerner, "knowing that if he did wipe out, or his equipment did falter, he would be eaten alive. And that's when that so-called J.A.W.S. image, Jaws came in. I told him, you don't even want to know what's behind you. It's Jaws" (*Laird* 2001, ch. 2).

Among disciples of big-wave surfing, Jaws is "the most perfect, top to bottom barreling, deadliest right in the world, and not one other wave comes close" (Doerner cited in *Laird* 2001, ch. 1). The break relies on more northerly swells than the big-wave breaks of O'ahu's North Shore. The island of Molokai blocks westerly swells from reaching Jaws, which has a swell window (i.e., the angles between a surf break and wave-producing depression that produce the best conditions for the particular site) of between 315 and 5 degrees. A massive trench, over 100 feet deep, caused by fresh water flowing out of the Pe'ahi Valley, sits on the western edge of the spur-shaped lava reef about half a mile from shore at Jaws. The reef, lying a mere 20 feet below the surface, refracts incoming waves into a classic bowl shape and causes the face to rise three to five times in height; Surfline calculates that Jaws can produce rideable wave faces of 95 feet (*Making the Call* 2003, ch. 4).

Since featuring in a highly praised sequence in Bruce Brown's *The Endless Summer II* (1994), a film otherwise generally rejected by critics, Jaws has appeared in numerous surf videos and DVDs including *Wake-up Call* (1995), *Liquid Thunder* (1999), *Biggest Wednesday* (1998), *Swell XXL*

Carlos Burle chased by Jaws during the XXL session on January 11, 2000.
Source: Tim McKenna.

(2001), and *Strapped* (2002). Laird Hamilton speaks reverentially of the wave's sheer power. He described being "vaporized" after an early wipeout at the break: "I felt like my body went into little particles" (Warshaw 2004, 302). One of the most spectacular wipeouts at Jaws occurred in 2002 when Ross Clarke-Jones fell under the lip. Film of the incident shows him turning head over heels down the face of the wave (*Making the Call* 2003, ch. 4); he also reported hitting the reef.

maverick's (california)

Described by Matt Warshaw (2000, front flap) as "ominous and intimidating," Maverick's, 25 miles south of San Francisco, at the northern end of Half Moon Bay, is widely regarded as one of the world's most powerful big-wave breaks. Local surfer Grant Washburn warns that the pitching lip of even a relatively small 15- to 20-foot wave at Maverick's "has the ability to rip your limbs off." He advises surfers to avoid the lip at all costs (*Making the Call* 2003, ch. 5). Indeed, the wave that killed Mark Foo at Maverick's in 1993 was an "unremarkable" 15-footer (Warshaw 2000, 172).

The swell window for Maverick's is wide, lying between 250 and 320 degrees, although the best swells come from the Gulf of Alaska to the northwest and travel around 1,500 miles. The shallow reef at Maverick's extends from the coast almost a mile out to sea. The south side of the reef drops quickly from 20 feet to over 80 feet. A series of alternating "steps" and channels line the reef at Maverick's; the steps jack the waves up, while the deeper water in the channels slows them. An outside ledge at Maverick's, beyond the main "theatre" closer to shore, causes waves with a face of 40 feet to feather. This ledge produces the best-shaped and biggest waves at Maverick's. In 2002 Carlos Burle won the XXL Big Wave Award Ride of the Year on a 68-footer that walled along the outside ledge. Surfline estimates that Maverick's could support a wave with an 85-foot face (*Making the Call* 2003, ch. 5).

In 1962 local Half Moon Bay surfer Alex Matienzo reconnoitered the reef with two friends. "That was the first and last time we surfed the place"; it was "too hard" and "too spooky," said Matienzo, adding that he named the break Maverick's Point after his German Shepherd dog. Thirteen years later, in February 1975, another local surfer, 17-year-old Jeff Clark, paddled out to Maverick's. "I'd seen the place breaking for a few years and in 1975 I finally got up the nerve to check it out. I tried to get people to paddle out there with me, but no one was interested. They all said, 'There's no way I'm going to paddle out there and drown. You go ahead, and I'll watch you from the channel.'" For the next 15 years Clark surfed Maverick's alone, although some winters passed without any swells. In December 1990 Clark was in San Francisco watching giant waves pound Ocean Beach when he met Tom Powers and Richard Schmidt, two surfers from Santa Cruz. Clark asked the pair "if they wanted to surf that swell in a perfect peak," and they tagged along with him to Maverick's where there were perfect waves breaking at 20 feet. "It looked like Waimea," Schmidt said. "I couldn't believe this place had been right under our noses for all these years." Powers and Schmidt paddled out for a closer look. "It was amazing," Powers said: "The meanest, sickest wave I'd ever seen." Clark now had company, which grew quickly over the following years (Quirarte 1998).

The lip is not the only danger at Maverick's. Adam Replogle warns that a whipping by the lip is only the beginning of a surfer's nightmare:

> You are going to have to deal with a couple more waves, and then these rocks...that are like a brick wall. [They] come up quickly and you have to think [quickly]: get your leash off, or pull your pin, get away from that board, find...I don't know how wide of a gap it is

between a couple of these rocks, thread the needle, and then sit in the bay, and count your blessings. And then, I've seen seals, [surfers] talk of sharks, people are getting bit[ten] out there, who knows what...else there is to deal with. So, if it isn't one thing that's going to get you, it's another. If you have a thin [heart] valve out there...pop. For sure. (*Making the Call* 2003, ch. 5)

In one session at Maverick's an avalanche of white water produced by a 40-foot wave devoured Greg Long; his subsequent hold down lasted 40 seconds and ruptured one of his eardrums (Thomas 2008).

outside log cabins (o'ahu)

Located about a mile north of Waimea Bay and nearly a mile offshore, Outside Log Cabins sits on the southern edge of the coral reef that extends around the North Shore of O'ahu. This section of the reef is also responsible for refracting waves shoreward and giving shape to those breaking closer to shore, including Pipeline. Dependent on huge North Pacific winter swells (within 2,000 miles and between 300 and 350 degrees [*Making the Call* 2003, ch. 3]), Outside Log Cabins begins to take form only at around 20 feet and is particularly fickle, revealing its full majesty perhaps two or three times a decade (Warshaw 2004, 437). Based on an analysis of the bathymetry, Surfline estimates that the largest possible wave at Outside Log Cabins could be around 90 feet on the face (*Making the Call* 2003, ch. 3).

In 1986 Ken Bradshaw and Trevor Sifon paddled-in to a 20-foot wave at Outside Log Cabins before being washed ashore by a 30-foot wave that caught them inside. Outside Log Cabins finally earned its reputation as a big-wave break on January 28, 1998, with the arrival of huge, "crystalline" waves generated by a deep depression 1,000 miles north of Hawai'i. The swell closed out all the beaches on the North Shore, including Waimea Bay where surfers had gathered for the Eddie Aikau memorial contest (see chapter 5); the organizers canceled the competition—it was impossible to get to the break (Jenkins 1998).

Most of the tow-in crew headed to the west side of O'ahu and Makaha and Makua Cave (Jenkins 1999, 182–83), but a dozen or so including Bradshaw and Dan Moore, Ross Clarke-Jones and Tony Ray, Cheyne Horan and Sam Hawk, Kawika Stant and Shawn Briley, and Noah Johnson and Aaron Lambert, punched their way through the shorebreak on their PWC.

the extreme north shore   The North Shore of O'ahu is perfectly positioned for extreme surf. Most of O'ahu's waves derive from winter storms in the northwest corner of the Pacific, off Japan (where warm, moist north-flowing air meets cold winds blowing off Asia). A large fetch (the distance that winds blow over water) of up to 1,500 miles in this part of the Pacific magnifies the size of waves. As waves move across the ocean they lose about 20 percent of their energy each day; the waves that reach O'ahu from the northwest Pacific travel only for one and a half to three days and thus they retain most of their energy.

Bradshaw made surfing history that day when Moore towed him into an 80-foot face. From the hills above the town of Pupukea, Bill Sickler, himself a big-wave veteran, watched Bradshaw surf what he described as "the most beautiful wave I've ever seen. Glassy and peeling, like Backdoor [see below] blown out of proportion. Ken was surfing beautifully. The gods were smiling on him. He couldn't do anything wrong" (Jenkins 1998). But the day did not belong only to Bradshaw. Cheyne Horan surfed the biggest waves he'd ever been in—"it didn't even look real" and "it felt like the whole planet was breaking"—and had "some exciting moments" including "going up to the top and snapping back as the lip was coming over on a [50-foot face]" (Jenkins 1998). One wave claimed Ross Clarke-Jones and Tony Ray and their PWC:

> On my fourth wave Tony put me in a little deep. We were going as fast as we could, and when I let go I was going faster than Tony, but neither of us were going fast enough. That [PWC] just couldn't outrun the wave. It collected me and Tony and we both got smashed. I popped up screaming, where the f**k is Tony. I couldn't see him anywhere and then I saw this patch of purple floating around. It was the seat of the [PWC]. I finally saw Tony a little further out than me. Tony and the [PWC] were getting dragged to the shore with the [PWC] full of water when Aaron Lambert came to the rescue. He towed Tony and the [PWC] back outside into the channel. (Jenkins 1998)

Film of the session at Outside Log Cabins appears in *The Moment* (1998), *Biggest Wednesday* (1998), and *Extreme* (1999).

pipeline (oʻahu)

Undoubtedly the most acclaimed wave in surfing, Pipeline "breaks with the precision of a guillotine" as the "swell jumps up on the shallow reef and pitches out to form a perfect tube" (Hemmings 1997, 53) that "spins and grinds for about seven seconds, tapering down the whole time" (Warshaw 2004, 463). Former world champion Barton Lynch (1991, 139) says that "for thrill, excitement and challenge the Pipeline is without comparison. Once ridden successfully, it makes most other waves fade into insignificance." Describing a ride at Pipeline, Mark Richards says the wave "completely closes over you and you're inside this huge, green barrel. Water is rushing and gurgling over your head and the whole ocean is shaking. All you can see is a little hole of sunlight at the end of the tube and you just hold your breath and pray it doesn't close before you get there" (Moses 1982, 87).

Located west of Ehukai Beach Park, Pipeline came to public attention with the release of Bruce Brown's *Surfing Hollow Days* (1962), which included a memorable scene of Phil Edwards dropping into an eight-foot Pipe barrel and "angling at high speed in the shadow of the curl" (Warshaw 2004, 178). Edwards claims to have surfed Pipeline alone the previous day and then returned to the site with Brown and fellow California surfer Mike Diffenderfer to film. Comparing the shape of the wave to an open trench he observed on the adjacent Kamehameha Highway, Diffenderfer proposed calling the break Pipeline (Warshaw 2004, 155).

Pipeline comprises three reefs:

First Reef, a flat lava plateau broken up by a few narrow crevasses and located less than 75 yards offshore, is the premier break. Second Reef Pipeline is located about 75 yards out from the regular Pipeline lineup, and comes into play when the surf hits 10 or 12 foot. Waves here often do little more than fringe along the crest, which allows the rider to make an early entry and set the ride up as the swell moves toward First Reef. Third Reef Pipeline, a shifty and foaming big-wave break located another 300 yards offshore, is rarely surfed. (Warshaw 2004, 463)

Classic Pipeline breaks left on a westerly swell. As the swell turns northwest, a right break, Backdoor, becomes rideable. For much of the year, however, Pipeline is unrideable. During summer months sand covers the reef, and it requires a few large winter swells to clear the reefs and allow the waves to assume their classic form (Lynch 1991, 137).

Very few surfers look truly comfortable riding Pipeline. Gerry Lopez was one, but even he insists that the wave rules: "You're always right on the edge at Pipeline; you're always hanging by your fingertips, you never really have it under control" (Warshaw 2004, 464). A 15-foot wave at Pipeline breaks with an estimated force of 1.4 tons per square foot; wipeouts catapult surfers into agitated waters that "rasp [them] against the coral" and whip them "like a rag doll with a fire hose trained on it." Resurfacing, riders often find themselves "suck[ing] in a lungful of foam"—the residue of the bygone set (Moses 1982, 88).

At Pipeline, injuries are frequent and deaths common. On December 3, 2005, Malik Joyeux, a "fearless big-wave surfer" from Tahiti who just two years earlier rode one of the biggest waves recorded at Teahupo'o (see below), died on a relatively tame eight-footer at Pipeline after falling and hitting the seabed (Doherty 2008, 8th moment).

Notwithstanding the dangers, the perfect symmetry of Pipeline continues to lure surfers—like it did Fred Van Dyke, who resigned from his teaching post in Santa Cruz and headed for O'ahu after seeing the 1953 photograph of Woody Brown, George Downing, and Buzzy Trent racing across a 15-foot wall at Makaha (chapter 2). Van Dyke subsequently became a big-wave rider and North Shore local (Grissim 1982, 35). Big Pipeline swells, which called to him at night in bed, lured him into the water until his late forties:

When the big waves come, they're at 15- to 18-second intervals. Boom! Shakes your house. Boom! Shakes your house. You know you've got to get some sleep, but you can't sleep because you hear that pounding, and you know you've got to meet it in the morning. When you get up you look out there and see the huge curls, and you look for excuses: It's too big, it's too windy, it's too choppy. But you know inside that it can be surfed. So, naturally you paddle out, and you're committed. You knew you had to do it. (Moses 1982, 90)

shipstern bluff (tasmania)

Unusual among big-wave sites with respect to the frequency with which it breaks, Shipstern Bluff, south of the notorious former convict settlement of Port Arthur and underneath a majestic bluff after which it takes

Steps on the face, inside the barrel, pose an extreme test of the surfer's skill. Kyle Davidson, The Island (New Zealand), 2004. *Source:* Mark Stevenson.

its name, can break as often as every two weeks in big Southern Ocean groundswells. Shipstern, however, is isolated—to get there requires a two-hour walk through national park forest and farmland or a trip by boat. Cold water—50 to 55 degrees Fahrenheit across the prime autumn-winter-spring season—and even colder air temperatures compound the isolation, as does the wave. At Shipstern the wave "doubles, even triples in size...as it rolls across the reef" and "huge steps" form on the wall; "the surfer needs to nail the bottom turn and set their angle before it hits the steps, otherwise they'll get sucked up the wave" (Barilotti 2002, 25). The step in the face of the wave is what makes Shipstern, in the words of triple world champion Andy Irons, "so out of bounds." As Irons explains, "it's so different to other heavy waves around the world, so twisted. It's so far from perfect and it's just looking for ways to f**k you up" (Doherty 2008, 47th moment).

While a handful of local surfers have reputedly been riding Shipstern on and off since the 1970s, the majority regarded it as "basically unsurfable." "We just thought it was some sort of cross between the Box and Shark Island," said local rider Chris Wescott (Carroll 2001). Shipstern finally achieved local acceptance in 2001 with the release of *Pulse,* a video by Justin Gane that featured "a fearful five-minute closing sequence of

David Rastovich and Brenden "Margo" Margieson getting pitted—and swiped—at [the break]." "After Ganey's video," says Wescott, "we went, 'Shit! It *is* surfable!" (Carroll 2001). *Pulse* attracted two surfaris organized by *Tracks*. The first, led by Matt Griggs, returned home pictureless; the second, led by Sean Davey and which included surfers Kieren Perrow, Mark Matthews, and Drew Courtney, produced visual and real drama. On the second day, a lip that wiped out Perrow revealed the full power of the wave, breaking his board lengthwise *and* crosswise (Doherty 2008, 20th moment).

Shipstern was now open for business, although, interestingly, the business nearly commenced a decade earlier when Graham Cassidy, the then-president of the Association of Surfing Professionals (ASP), visited Tasmania with Mark Richards in an effort to encourage local tourism authorities to co-sponsor a World Qualifying Series contest. Five years later, in 1996, Cassidy returned with a view to organizing another contest; this time he even reconnoitered Shipstern.

> We checked it out twice, but only saw it once when there was a taste of what it could be like. We went out in boats and surveyed the whole site and went, "Oh God, this is incredible." Nobody was surfing. It's pretty haunting stuff. The rock is so chunky and sharp, you start thinking about the possibility of something going wrong out there. (Carroll 2001)

Indeed, surfing Shipstern is very much about survival, as the June 2006 double-cover issue of *Tracks* graphically illustrates. The first cover features a photograph of a cold, "nasty" Shipstern wave, with a ruffled, dissected, and uneven face in a state of collapse. The headline calls it "The Beast," although the caption describes it more aesthetically as a "15ft [Salvador] Dali painting." On the collapsing wall is a crouching Andy Irons who is clearly running the gauntlet of raw ocean power. The feeling of the image is pure menace. The second cover features a photograph from the same session. Sitting on top of the caption "Hell Kid: Laurie Towner's Wave of the Year," the photograph shows Towner standing poised under a perfectly formed, spinning, curved Shipstern lip (see chapter 3). The second cover is a gatefold that opens to a 14-shot sequence of Towner's ride. But it's all predictably short-lived at Shipstern for Towner; the traditional "back page" photograph shows Towner "bodybashed" by tons of Shipstern white water. Recounting this thrashing at the break, Towner described his foot slipping as he rose to his board: "I just kinda dived off and started bodysurfing. I just got *sooo* snapped. [I]t sucked me up then I actually fell through the top of the barrel and hit the bottom—then it sucked me over again" (Phillips 2006, 118).

teahupo'o (tahiti)

Teahupo'o has assumed the mantle of the world's most powerful and ferocious wave. Two-time world surfing champion Tom Carroll describes it as a "Garden of Eden,...the most serene, most beautiful, most raw place in the world," but "all of a sudden, it will just come alive...out of the middle of nowhere, it will deliver the most serious wave you have ever seen, [breaking] down the reef like a guillotine" (Blackwater 2005, ch. 4). The power and ferocity of the wave, says legendary waterman Brian Keaulana (son of Buffalo Keaulana), comes from the weight and mass of water behind it: "The back of the wave? There is no back; it's the whole ocean behind that thing" (*Billabong Odyssey* 2003, ch. 11).

On the southwest coast of Tahiti, Teahupo'o sits at a break in the reef caused by fresh water flowing out of an entire valley and cutting through the coral like a knife. The "magic of Teahupo'o," says Sean Collins, Surfline's chief forecaster, lies in its extreme marine contour, which rises, in a mere 300 feet, from about 150 feet deep to 3 feet. This radical variance causes the wave to literally appear out of nowhere and suddenly stand up. In addition, the swell bends sharply at the pass in the reef and the faster-moving swell pushes water in front of the walling face; the wave thus takes on the appearance of a huge slab of ocean. Without a back, the wave crashes like a concrete slab onto the reef. The best swells for Teahupo'o come from the direct south—generated by low pressure systems east of the South Island of New Zealand and enable the wave to run down the reef. Southerly swells also give surfers a little more warning of the approaching waves compared with the squarer-hitting southwest swells (generated south of Australia and travelling through the Tasman Sea). Under the latter conditions, a 20-foot wave can suddenly appear directly in front of a surfer with virtually no warning. "It can be a little bit spooky," says Collins, in a classic understatement (*Blackwater* 2005, ch. 6). Having a "monstrous closeout charge you" at Teahupo'o engenders real fear, admits professional surfer Kieren Perrow: "You can't even think about duckdiving a big one. I've learnt the hard way...you will end up going backwards over a waterfall into a dry reef" (Perrow 2009, 30).

The name Teahupo'o means "wall of heads"; after beating their neighbors in a bloody war, the victors cut off the heads of their defeated enemies and used the skulls to construct a wall, reputedly to demarcate their territory (*Blackwater* 2005, ch. 4). According to local history, Vaheatooa, a female whose name meant "the idol of god," surfed the break at Havae Pass outside Teahupo'o, which she called "Pererue." Vaheatooa rode the waves at Pererue alone. The chief of Teahupo'o, jealous of her surfing skill, killed her, believing he would assume Vaheatooa's surfing skills. But the chief failed to conquer Pererue (*Blackwater* 2005, ch. 4).

In more contemporary times, Timothee Faraires and his two brothers from Vairoa, about 10 minutes inland, began riding Teahupo'o in the early 1980s. According to Timothee, he took one of his brothers to Teahupo'o in 1982 because neither felt comfortable surfing the break alone (*Blackwater* 2005, ch. 4). It is a consistent refrain: local professional surfer Alain Riou recalls going there as teenager when it was six to eight feet and nobody was there. He would "look around for half an hour," "get scared," and leave to surf in front of the village (*Blackwater* 2005, ch. 4). Surfers dribbled through over the next decade until 1994 when Eric Barton appeared riding Teahupo'o on the July cover of *Surfer;* the photograph revealed the wave's potential and opened it to the international surfing community.

Teahupo'o became a contest site on the World Championship Tour (WCT) in 1999 after two years as a location on the World Qualifying Series. Twelve-foot-plus waves in the 1998 contest alerted the ASP and sponsors to the break's potential as a major venue. Koby Abberton won that year: "I knew I could win," Abberton later said, recalling his victory:

> I wasn't scared to drown, I wasn't scared to die or whatnot, and everyone else was. On my mind was 12 grand and I want to win, I want that. I don't care what I have to go through to get it. I'd luckily caught three really big, good waves in the final, come out on top. It opened a lot of doors for me. (Jones 2005)

Gotcha sponsored the first two WCT contests; Billabong has been the sponsor since 2001.

As noted in chapter 3, and implicit in Abberton's comments above, Teahupo'o raises questions about the conditions under which professional surfers should compete. At Teahupo'o the surfers demand quality rescue and medical facilities and feel a lot more comfortable with the presence of the Tahitian water patrol. According to Perry Hatchett, a former head judge on the WCT, there is a constant vigilance to "gauge whether it is possible for the surfers to paddle-in to the wave. Once it starts to get over 12 feet with a west swell it's nearly impossible" (*Blackwater* 2005, ch. 11). With a tone of relief in his voice, contest director Chris O'Callaghan says so far there have been no "totally major" incidents, but he admits to "feeling we are only one contest away from a real tragedy" (*Blackwater* 2005, ch. 11). In 2000 at Teahupo'o, Laird Hamilton rode what some have described as the wave of the millennium, a slab with a 20-foot face and a 10-foot-thick lip (see chapter 5).

todos santos (mexico)

Located in Baja California, around 60 miles south of the U.S. border and about 8 miles off the coast of Ensenada, is Todos Santos Island (All Saints Island) and a break known as Killers. A former editor of *Surfer* and *Surfing* and an accomplished big-wave rider in his own right, Evan Slater describes Killers (henceforth Todos Santos) as a "smaller," "more playful version of Waimea" (see below). It has "a steep drop and one quick section," like Waimea (Long 1999, 121; Casey 2010, ch. 8). In February 1998 Taylor Knox rode a 52-foot face at Todos Santos while competing in the semifinals of the Big Wave World Championship. Although Knox did not win the contest (which was won by Carlos Burle), he did win $50,000 in a Big Wave Challenge sponsored by the ski and snowboard manufacturer K2. This was the first contest in which judges based their decision on photographs of the wave (Warshaw 2004, 639; *Making the Call* 2003, ch. 6).

Surfers had been intermittently riding smaller surf in the immediate vicinity of Killers since the early 1960s. The break briefly became known as the biggest wave in North America in the late 1980s—before the discovery of Maverick's—after *Surfing* featured it in a 1987 article. The article, titled simply "Big Time" and written by professional surfer Dave Parmenter, dramatically captured the first set of the first recorded big-wave session at Todos Santos:

> Reaching the lineup during a lull, we positioned ourselves relative to the boils from the last set. A set approached off the point, a huge Waimea-like wall that refracted and accelerated with the curve of the headland into a jacking Sunset Beach peak. The sheer mass of the waves was unlike anything I have ever seen outside of Hawaii. I took

measuring the big ones Judges in big-wave awards examine enhanced photographs (and film where available). They measure the height of the wave between the lip and the trough at the highest moment during the ride. The distance between the surfer and the lip is usually easier to measure than that between the surfer and the bottom of the trough. The latter refers to the lowest point at which either the rider or the white water of the broken wave would be expected to reach. Judges in big-wave awards increasingly find themselves torn between awarding prizes to surfers who ride the biggest face and those who ride smaller but infinitely more deadly slabs of ocean.

the first wave, testing the fin placement with the longest bottom-turn I could muster to evade a very frisky end-bowl. Kicking out, I watched Tom [Curren] swing it around at the last second on an even bigger wave. A skipping drop, high compression bottom-turn, a two-G top turn, and he was back in the channel.... Out the back Chris [Burke] had the lineup to himself. A wave approached that seemed to possess the very soul of the devil. [H]e bull-dogged to his feet as this beast of a wave was already pitching, and somehow hung on beneath the vaulting lip long enough to beat it to the trough. From there he fought a losing battle with forty feet of churning soup. (Parmenter 1987, 94 and 97)

Todos Santos enjoys wide exposure to swells from the west and northwest, but the best swell window lies between 260 and 290 degrees and the waves break only a couple of times each year. The Gulf of Alaska generates the best swells. An underwater canyon forms a trench just off the northwest tip of the island. Mike Parsons, "the unofficial mayor of Todos" (Duane 1998b), describes the wave at Todos Santos as jacking straight up. Although it lacks the power, and the wall, of Jaws and Maverick's, Parsons says it will "get your attention if you fall" (*Making the Call* 2003, ch. 6). During the Billabong Odyssey, Billabong's three-year search for the biggest waves ever ridden, a large wave at Todos Santos caught Skindog Collins and slammed him into the impact zone:

It just buried me. When the thing hit me it was like a Mack [truck]. It hit me so hard and fast my back felt like it completely toppled in; my feet hit me in the head. And then that thing just racked on me for a couple of hundred yards. (*Billabong Odyssey* 2003, ch. 5)

Surfline estimates that the largest surfable wave at Todos would be around 85 feet on the face (*Making the Call* 2003, ch. 3).

waimea (oʻahu)

From the late 1950s until the early 1990s, with the advent of tow-in surfing and the discovery of Maverick's, Waimea was the shrine of big-wave surfing, although the rides are generally short—around 10 seconds—and characterized by near-vertical take-offs. Former world champion Shaun Thomson describes Waimea as "survival—the straight line death drop to the bottom, ignite afterburners, hard square turn to safety. Sometimes there is space for a slash off the top, and sometimes even a tube for the totally committed" (Brady 1983, 42). Brock Little's tube during the Eddie Aikau memorial contest (see chapter 5) in 1990, in which he rode deep inside the bowels of a 35-footer and came out unscathed, drew acclaim for years (Duane 1998a):

> I took off sort of behind the peak and it was either go straight and get nailed or just pull up into the tube. So, I pulled up into the tube, and wow; it was a monster, a beast. I was just so deep. I couldn't believe I got tubed at Waimea Bay; I got barreled. (*The Mountain and the Wave* 2006, ch. 8)

Little also suffered a heavy wipeout during the contest. Hitting the water, his body failed to penetrate and he skipped over the surface underneath the collapsing white water, which quickly caught up and threw him into the "washing machine": "My arm went one way, my leg went another way,...you just don't know what's going on" (*The Mountain and the Wave* 2006, ch. 8).

Unlike other big-wave sites, Waimea Bay prefers shorter swell periods of about 15 seconds (swells with longer periods tend to shoal on the reefs farther north at Outside Log Cabins—see above). The swell window for Waimea Bay lies between 300 and 340 degrees, with the best swells originating about 1,200 miles northwest of Oʻahu centered around latitude 40°–45° north and longitude 180° west (*Making the Call* 2003, ch. 2); more northerly swells soften the take-off and produce a longer wall compared with the steeper take-offs but shorter walls of the westerly swells (Warshaw 2004, 676).

As 20-foot swells approach Waimea they rise quickly over a very shallow ledge to create critical drops of 30 to 50 feet; the middle of the bay is deeper due to the flow of fresh water out of the Waimea Valley cutting into rock and coral over thousands of years. Once the waves reach about 50 feet on the face at Waimea, the ledge ceases to have an effect and the wave breaks in the bay. Surfline estimates that the largest face at Waimea is probably about 55 feet (*Making the Call* 2003, ch. 2).

Many of the legendary sessions at Waimea have been associated with competitions, particularly since the launch of the Eddie Aikau memorial contest. The Smirnoff contest, which ran for nine years from 1969 and was considered one of surfing's key events, undoubtedly gained its reputation in 1974 when the final four heats were held in 25-foot-plus surf at Waimea Bay. Mark Richards, who was then just 17 years old, was a contestant. He remembers contest director Fred Hemmings pressuring surfers to compete:

> A lot of the guys who had experience in Hawai'i were questioning the sanity of actually running the event. And Fred Hemmings basically said, "Look, you guys are a bunch of wusses. I'll paddle out there and catch a wave and prove it can be ridden." As soon as he said that, everyone knew it was going to be on because we knew Fred would actually do it. (Coleman 2004, 136)

Several extreme wipeouts marked the contest. Barry Kanaiaupuni and James Jones suffered particularly wrenching wipeouts. Kanaiaupuni "bounced down" the face of one wave, which proceeded to "devour him and destroy his board. After almost drowning on the way in, he got pounded in the shorebreak (Coleman 2004, 136–37). Jones took off on one of the larger waves of the contest:

> I got half-way down the face, and I hit a big chop, and the board broke in half while I was still standing on it. I got slammed. I fell face first into the water. The worst part of a wipeout on a big wave like that is when you hit the water; the impact kind of stuns you, if it doesn't knock you out. I came up, and I was numb on one side of my body. I couldn't use that arm or leg. I was semi-conscious, floating around in the impact zone, and there was another wave coming....I thought, "Shit,...I'm gonna drown in front of 10,000 people." (Coleman 2004, 138)

The first person to assist Jones was Eddie Aikau. As he paddled toward Jones, Aikau took a large leather strap from around his shoulders and on reaching the stricken surfer held the strap out. Jones grabbed the strap with his functioning arm and Aikau brought Jones in almost to the beach through a series of blasting waves (Coleman 2004, 138).

Reno Abellira won the 1974 Smirnoff contest, the finals of which *Tracks* later described as "the most spectacular day in surfing history" (Warshaw 2004, 548).

There are, of course, many other extreme surfing breaks around the globe (e.g., Aileens, Ireland; Cow Bombie, Western Australia; Egypt, Maui; Ghost Trees, California; Papatowai, New Zealand; Pedra Branca, Tasmania) as well as others still waiting to be discovered. Fickleness is a recurring theme in discussions of extreme surf breaks, and patience, a keen eye, and luck are essential prerequisites for discovering new sites. Jamie Mitchell and Billy Watson monitored one reef off the east coast of Australia and studied swell charts and weather maps for years before they eventually scored a memorable session—seven and a half hours of over-head to double-overhead "plate glass perfection"—at a break they named Krispy Kremes (a wave as round as a donut). Four days later, with a seem-ingly identical swell and wind they returned to the break to find the "do-nuts" replaced by "burgers" (Watson 2009, 94). Jeff Clark–type souls are undoubtedly jealously guarding breaks that they enjoy surfing alone. But as I have demonstrated in this chapter, surfers are explorers, and sooner or later *the* spot comes to wider attention. Moreover, the paradox of surfing is that the rider must be seen before he or she can forge a reputation, and to this end secrecy is self defeating. With this in mind, it is to reputations and heroes that I now turn.

5.　heroes

I came charging in on a comber. As I neared the beach, there, in the water, up to her waist, dead in front of me, appeared a woman. How was I to stop that comber on whose back I was? It looked like a dead woman. The board weighed seventy-five pounds, I weighed a hundred and sixty-five. The added weight had a velocity of fifteen miles per hour. The board and I constituted a projectile. I leave it to the physicists to figure out the force of the impact upon that...woman....I steered with my legs, I steered sharply, abruptly, with all my legs and with all my might. The board sheered around broadside on the crest....The wave gave me...a tap sufficient to knock me off the board and smash me down through the rushing water to bottom....I got my head out for a breath of air and then gained my feet. There stood the woman before me. I felt like a hero. I had saved her life.

Jack London (1911, 74–75)

chasing swells and riding waves is, for many surfers, a lifestyle that differentiates and separates them from nonsurfers and draws them into a form of community. A surfing lifestyle, however, does not translate into a harmonious community (Barnes 1995, 147). On the contrary, as Max Weber, one of the founding fathers of sociology, recognized, "*competitors* who continue to compete" are the building blocks of communities (Barnes 1995, 147). What do members of lifestyle communities compete for? In a nutshell, they compete for prestige and for peer recognition of their worth, merit, and status. Social theorists agree that prestige constitutes "a prime force in human society" (Goldschmidt 1992, 48; see also Barkow 1975 and Goode 1978). In his analysis of heroes, William Goode describes prestige as a "system of social control that shapes much of social life." "All people," Goode (1978, vii) says,

81

share the universal need to gain the respect and esteem of others, since without it they cannot as easily elicit the help of others, and all individuals and groups give and withhold prestige and approval as a way of rewarding or punishing others. The foundations of social life rest in part on the universal need for respect, esteem, approval and honor.

The surfing community, of course, allocates prestige and establishes hierarchies of status according to performances on waves.

By the early 1950s surfers were organizing competitions as a formal means to rank status. Yet, while the best competitive surfers undoubtedly earn the respect of their peers, the spirituality, freedom, and artistry of riding waves leaves many surfers ambivalent about contests and awarding points for specific maneuvers. Renowned Australian big-wave rider Bob Pike expressed his concerns in the 1950s:

I don't like to compete and I don't think any of the top board riders do. It takes too much of the pleasure out of the sport and creates too many jealousies. Competitions are all against the spirit of surfing which is supposed to be a communion with nature rather than a hectic chase for points. ("Australia's Fifty" 1992, 88)

Even Graham Cassidy, a key figure in the development of professional surfing and a president of the Association of Surfing Professionals, expressed doubts: "deep in my subconscious I have this reluctance to be part of competitive surfing. I'm racked with these fears...that what I'm doing is going to take away from surfing the virtues that first attracted me" (Jarratt 1977b). However, it did not take long before the rewards of professionalism and a professional contest circuit became apparent even to the least competitive surfers who recognized that organized, well-publicized competition paradoxically offered a route to eternal hedonism, a means to finance an exotic lifestyle based on riding the best waves around the globe.

Irrespective of their rank in professional competition, surfers continue to reserve the highest prestige for those who prove themselves in extreme conditions and perform on extreme waves. Kelly Slater may have won six world championships and Andy Irons back-to-back world titles, says *Surfer* editor Scott Bass (2004a), but "their exploits combined pale in comparison" to those of Laird Hamilton, who "rode the unrideable at Teahupoo" and "ripped the unrippable at Pe'ahi." Riding extreme surf, explains former *Tracks* editor Sean Doherty, requires outstanding ability and, no less important, the right "mental aptitude": "You've got to have a brain that will allow you to take off on a wave like that. And that's where these guys differ from average surfers" (*Bra Boys* 2006, ch. 14). In these words Doherty identifies what sociologists call personal prowess, an attribute I introduced in chapter 1.

Some sociologists define personal prowess as "a quality that entail[s] skill, muscular strength, and endurance combined with an appreciation of strategy, or what Homer called cunning," and ambition as "the will to excel and to assert oneself in the pursuit of personal glory and fame" (Morford and Clarke 1976, 167–68). But prowess and ambition are not enough to achieve recognition and honor. The essential ingredient of status and prestige is "courage." In surfing, courage comes to the fore in confronting massive walls of water, especially those that break on shallow reefs, and dropping down vertical faces. Randy Rarick, executive director of the Triple Crown of Surfing, places courage at the center of personal prowess and status in the surfing community:

> Never in my life have I had more fear than being faced with a 25-foot wall of water bearing down on me and looking 50 feet into the pit while stroking into a vertical takeoff. Yet, nowhere else have I ever experienced the sheer excitement, rush and nearly indescribable feeling of elation in making a giant wave. While the continued growth of the pro-surfing tour will produce dramatic advances in the sport, [there will be people] out there on the North Shore seeking the ultimate thrill and reaffirming that *real* men ride big waves. (Brady 1983, 48)

Courage and personal prowess also translate into a form of power that has the ability to command. Accounts of such power ripple through stories of extreme surfing. Ricky Grigg recalls the early years of big-wave riding in Oʻahu as the pastime started to get "competitive":

> You got damn scared at times. You got so scared you needed each other to do what you were doing. I've been real scared at Waimea. . . . I've taken off on waves at Waimea that I probably wouldn't have, had Greg Noll not been watching. (Noll and Gabbard 1989, 146)

The "single most electrifying" event renowned surfer Jeff Hakman observed during his competitive career occurred in giant surf at Waimea Bay just prior to the semifinals of the 1974 Smirnoff contest (see chapter 4). Hakman and his fellow competitors were in the water, waiting for judges to commence the contest, when a monstrous wave approached. A young local, "T-Bone," started paddling:

> The wave just jacked up and it was huge. It started to suck him up the face and he was at the moment of commitment. We were all so close we could see the expression on his face. He...faltered his paddling rhythm for a split second and I could tell he was wondering. Suddenly we're yelling...at him to go, go! I'll never forget that look on his face, a mixture of apprehension and pride. [W]hat's he gonna do? Every surfer in the world that he respects and admires is watching him. Suddenly he's hanging there in space...he just plunged, fell out of the sky, landed on his board and the both of them got sucked back over the falls again. There was a split second where he knew he wasn't going to make that wave and where he could have pulled back, but he didn't. He pushed it too far, but he knew he had to or it wasn't worth a damn thing. (Jarratt 1997, 125)

Commands to exhibit courage and prowess are not always direct orders. When young surfer Tom Rudd reached the water's edge at Pipeline on a dull, gloomy morning, he confronted ugly, uneven 10- to 12-foot waves. But Rudd knew he had no options. A guest in the bunkroom of Volcom House, "home to some of Pipe's most fearless surfers" who are "as hard as the...reef...and similarly uncompromising," Rudd understood he had to paddle out to earn peer respect (Doherty 2008, 6th moment).

Sociologist and surfer Clif Evers (2004, 36) refers to the embodiment of prowess and courage. He describes one particular "charger," with whom he shared a session, as having "muscular arms" and a "barrel chest" and exhibiting a conspicuous demeanor of "nonchalance." Nearly every article on Laird Hamilton makes reference to his energy and his commanding

---

all shapes and sizes   Extreme surfers come in all shapes and sizes. At one extreme are Laird Hamilton (6'3", 215 lbs.) and Greg Noll (6'2", 230 lbs.). At the other end of the spectrum are Darrick Doerner (5'6", 140 lbs.) and the slightly taller but lighter Mark Foo (5'8", 135 lbs.). Ten-time world champion and winner of the big-wave Eddie Aikau memorial contest, Kelly Slater is a very average five nine, 160 pounds.

size and presence. Scott Bass (2004a) describes him as "a unique amalgamation of pioneer test pilot and waterman, a sort of Chuck Yeager meets Duke Kahanamoku," and Michael Fordham (2008, 232) calls him a "statue of Moses." Ben Marcus (2009, 102) is the least rhetorical: his Laird is just "fit, tan, rugged, tall, blonde and handsome." At the other end of the spectrum, "kooks"—blithering beginners disconnected from the rhythms of the ocean and its waves—lack embodied style. Kooks hold their arms "as if there is a watermelon under each," and they "lock" their torsos (Doherty and Mondy 2005, 81).

Each generation of modern surfers has produced a crop of big-wave riders who have earned reputations for exceptional prowess and courage. The honor rolls include:

- '50 and '60s: Jose Angel, Peter Cole, Pat Curren, George Downing, Ricky Grigg, Greg Noll, Buzzy Trent, and Fred Van Dyke
- '70s and '80s: Reno Abellira, Clyde Aikau, Eddie Aikau, Ian Cairns, Mike Doyle, Jeff Hakman, James Jones, Barry Kanaiaupuni, Gerry Lopez, Mark Richards, Shaun Tomson, Jock Sutherland, and Nat Young
- '90s and '00s: Koby Abberton, Ken Bradshaw, Carlos Burle, Ross Clarke-Jones, Darrick Doerner, Laird Hamilton, Noah Johnson, Dave Kalama, Brock Little, Greg Long, Mark Foo, Mark Matthews, Garrett McNamara, and Mike Parsons

In this chapter I identify and discuss Greg Noll, Eddie Aikau, and Laird Hamilton as shining examples of each generation. Noll, Aikau, and Hamilton personify the valor and verve of extreme surfing. Beforehand, however, I introduce Miki "Da Cat" Dora, who embodied another type of hero in surfing culture: the "outlaw." While outlaw is an ambiguous term, *Tracks* editor Luke Kennedy (2009a, 10) defines the surfing outlaw as a "cult figure who seamlessly blazes an alternative path," and in this sense Dora is "surfing's definitive outlaw figure" (Warshaw 2004, 160).

miki "da cat" dora (1934–2002)

Exceptionally light on his feet and able to draw impeccably smooth and flawlessly elegant lines across the face of the wave, "Da Cat" established his reputation for "extreme behavior" around Malibu in the 1950s and '60s (Fisher 2007, 85). His exploits included firing army surplus rockets from

Malibu pier, painting swastikas on his boards, and dropping his board-shorts and "mooning" the judging panel while riding a wave in the 1967 Malibu Invitational contest. In a particularly controversial act, Dora adopted a crucified position on a cross made of two surfboards in an advertisement for his Da Cat signature Greg Noll Surfboard. With his troops in tow, Dora "blitzkrieged countless society functions, cinema premiers, political events and bohemian soirees" (Stecyk and Kampion 2005, 39).

The increasing popularization of surfing, particularly after 1962, destroyed Dora's idyllic existence at Malibu (Stecyk and Kampion 2005, 42–43). He responded by railing against the commercialization of surfing—of which he was a financial beneficiary—as well as "kooks of all colors, fags, finks, ego heroes, Amen groupies and football-punchy Valley swingers" whom he accused of invading his playground (Warshaw 2004, 161).

Dora also had a penchant for petty theft. In 1969 he forged a credit card, which supported a two-year spending spree. In 1973 police arrested and charged Dora with fraud for using a bad check to buy skis. He appeared in court in late 1974 and received three years probation. Dora violated the conditions of his probation and the court issued a warrant for his arrest. He left the country and was arrested in France in 1981 and extradited back to the United States where he was remanded in custody. Dora finally faced court in 1982, and in addition to three years probation he received another 161 days in a county jail. While in jail he was charged with crimes relating to his fraudulent use of a credit card between 1969 and 1971. Facing a 10-year sentence, Dora plea-bargained and received a much lighter six-month term. He was finally released in mid-December 1982 (Stecyk and Kampion 2005, 92 and 94).

Like Laird Hamilton, Dora had a corporeal presence and style that "relegated everyone and everything else to mere second fiddle." At Malibu

---

greg noll on miki dora   "Da Cat...was one of the most interesting and challenging people I have ever known. ...Mickey [*sic*] was a genius, certainly in surfing. The difficulty he had in everyday life was that he truly saw things from a different perspective than the average person. Consequently, he reacted to many of life's challenges in ways many people just couldn't understand" (cited in Kampion 2007, 110).

he "walked the beach with a contemptuous authority, with a peculiar cant and shuffling cadence that was unique." Dora's "disregard" made everyone else "seem common and dull, and somehow subjugated" (Stecyk and Kampion 2005, 8). His fellow surfers revered him. Greg Noll called him "a genius" (Noll and Gabbard 1989, 129); Nat Young said he was "the sanest person I knew. Total sanity" (Stecyk and Kampion 2005, 106). The mainstream press variously described him as a "renegade spirit" (*New York Times*), a "dark prince of the beach" (*Vanity Fair*) and "a hero to a generation of beach bums" (*Times,* London) (Rensin 2008, front flap). Historians of the sport refer to him as "surfing's Muhammad Ali" (Kampion 1997, 84), a "black knight" (Kennedy 2009b, 36), and "a romantic Robin Hood of surfing" (Steve Pezman cited in Rensin 2008, 20). Elaborating on his description, Pezman says Dora was

> important to all of us who were living traditional, canned, commodified lives because he was a larger-than-life figure who somehow lived our dream for us. He expressed everything—athletically, politically and emotionally—that we couldn't express ourselves. He was the rebel spirit who flipped-off society and went his own way. (cited in Rensin 2008, 20)

Surfing was Dora's "escape" and his life a series of waves into which he "dropped," "set up," "pulled into" and went for "broke":

> And behind me, all the shit goes over my back—the screaming parents, screaming teachers, police, priests, politicians, kneeboarders, windsurfers, they're all going over the falls head-first into the reef, head-first into the f**king reef, waaah. I'm shooting for my life and when it starts to close out I pull out and [paddle] back out to pick up another one or two and do the same goddamn thing. (*Surfers: The Movie* 2008)

"Dora Lives" graffiti perennially reappears on the wall at Malibu which demarcates "the pit" where the early Malibu core congregated.

Dora had no interest in big surf, preferring waves around 4 feet (Warshaw 2004, 161). However, when he accepted a position as a stunt rider in *Ride the Wild Surf* (1964) he was ordered into 20-foot waves at Waimea. Clearly uncomfortable and "shaky," Dora nonetheless earned Greg Noll's plaudits. Dora, said Noll, was the only surfer he knew who was capable of making the transition from Malibu to Waimea in one session (Noll and Gabbard 1989, 131).

greg noll (1937–)

The legendary big-wave rider who worked as lifeguard, surfboard maker, surfing-film cinematographer, professional surfer, and fisherman, Greg Noll was a member of a lifeguard team from the United States that toured Australia in 1956 and introduced the Malibu surfboard, which helped precipitate the surfing craze "down under."

Noll quickly established his reputation as a big-wave rider among the first generation to tackle the North Shore of Oʻahu. His name became inextricably linked with Waimea Bay, a break he called "my girl":

> I surfed with this beautiful woman, who allowed me to get away with shit as long as I didn't act too outrageously towards her. There were times when the surf would get perfect.... You'd go out and catch a wave, and just make this thing, and have your adrenaline dripping out of your ear and you'd paddle out, do it again. You'd get a little cocky—get your arse slapped a little bit—she'd let you know it. But for the most part, it was just this full-on love affair that took place for 25 years. (*Riding Giants* 2004, ch. 8)

In November 1964 Noll rode a memorable 25-foot wave at Outside Pipeline. After battling the shorebreak for the best part of an hour with Mike Stange, Noll reached the far reef at Pipeline where "there were no lineups" and "nothing to indicate what our positions should be." "The wave I caught...that day," says Noll,

> walled up 25 feet about half a mile in front of me. Instead of getting smaller as I rode it, the sonofabitch grew on me. It just kept getting bigger and bigger, and I started going faster and faster until I was absolutely locked into it. I felt like I was on a spaceship racing into a void. At first I could hear my board chattering across the face of the wave in a constant rhythm. As my speed increased, the chattering noise became less frequent. Suddenly there was no noise. For about 15 or 20 feet, I was airborne. Then I literally was blown off my board. When I hit and went underwater, I thought I was going to drown. I got pounded good before I popped up and started sweating the next wave. (Noll and Gabbard 1989, 138)

Surf photographer and filmmaker Bud Browne filmed Noll's wave, which appeared in *Locked In* (1964). However, his ride on a 35-foot wave at Makaha on December 4, 1969—a feat immortalized by Ken Auster in his widely reproduced serigraph *Makaha 1969*—cemented Noll's status as a legend.

Noll grew up at Manhattan Beach, California, where he learned to surf in 1948 at age 11. His first surfboard was solid redwood and weighed over 100 pounds. He spent the entire first summer trying to catch a wave. Noll began regularly visiting Hawai'i while still a schoolboy. In 1954 he temporarily moved to the islands, where he lived in a Quonset hut at Makaha, spending most of his time surfing, diving, and fishing. Returning to the mainland, he left school and shaped surfboards while working part-time as a lifeguard. Initially operating out of a garage, Noll's surfboard-making business grew quickly, and he opened a small shop at Manhattan Beach. He later moved to a larger shop at Hermosa Beach before building a combined surfboard factory and shop at Hermosa in 1965. Due to intense business competition, he closed the factory in 1971.

Noll has provided a graphic account of his experience at Makaha in the swell of 1969 when he paddled into, took off, rode, and then wiped out on the 35-foot face:

> Finally a set came thundering down....
>
>   ...I caught a glimpse of my wave....I turned and began paddling, hard. I felt a rush of adrenalin as the wave approached, lifted me and my board began to accelerate. Then I was on my feet, committed.
>
>   You could have stacked two eighteen-wheel semis on top of each other against the face of that wave and still have had room left over to ride it. [M]y board began to howl like a goddamn jet....
>
>   I flew down the face, past the lip of the wave, and when I got to the bottom...I looked ahead and saw the sonofabitch starting to break in a section that stretched a block and a half in front of me....The wave threw out a sheet of water over my head and engulfed me.
>
>   My board flew out from under me. I hit the water going so fast that it was like hitting concrete....[T]ons of whitewater exploded over me. It pounded me under. It thrashed and rolled me beneath the surface until my lungs burned and there was so much pressure that I felt my eardrums were going to burst....[T]he whitewater finally began to dissipate and the turbulence released me. I made it to the surface, gulped for air and quickly looked outside. There was another monster, heading my way. (Noll and Gabbard 1989, 7–8)

A sense of letdown overwhelmed Noll after his exploit, and shortly afterward he ceased going to Hawai'i. The period coincided with the death of his stepfather, Ash, and mounting economic pressures and the closure of his surfboard factory. He sold the shop and returned briefly to working as a lifeguard before departing for Alaska where he became a commercial fisherman for the next decade and a half: "I just wanted to find some place quiet where I could enjoy my family, play with the kids, swim in the ocean and do some hunting and fishing" (Noll and Gabbard 1989, 175). Interestingly because the story is similar, Ken Bradshaw descended into a state of depression after riding a colossal wave at Outside Log Cabins in 1998 (see chapter 4).

> Being at Outside Logs was something I'd dreamed about, planned for, thought about, for almost 20 years. All of a sudden it happened. And then it was gone. It was such a high, so fulfilling, life after that was just anticlimactic. I was like, wow...now what? For the first time, I got a handle on that Greg Noll thing. (Jenkins 1999, 179)

More recently Noll has returned to the surfing scene, shaping reproductions of original Hawai'ian surfboards. He is a lauded elder of the surfing community, a peer of peers who led the charge into surfing's extreme realm.

eddie aikau (1946–1978)

"A gentle monster of big wave surfing, a Waimea Emperor, a straight up, full-blooded surfing immortal" (Warshaw 2005/06, 91), Edward Ryon Aikau began surfing at age 11. He made a spectacular debut at Waimea Bay on November 19, 1967, riding giant waves with precision for over six hours without leaving the water. Peter Cole vividly remembers Eddie "charging right off the bat....It was a really big day. He took off on as big a wave as anyone was taking off on. I'd say the bigger sets were [30-foot-plus faces], but it was so clean and consistent." In one photograph from the session, Aikau, who wore red and white boardshorts and rode a big red Hobie surfboard, is standing with his arms spread out and his legs bent on a face six times his height and just under the curling lip (Coleman 2004, 55–60). Big-wave surfer Darrick Doerner described Aikau's style as "take off and drop in, big bottom turn, disappear into a mountain of whitewater, pop out, throw his hair back" (Warshaw 2004, 7). Ken Bradshaw regarded

Eddie Aikau as a hero. After introducing Bradshaw to Waimea (Martin 2007, 75), Aikau continued his mentorship, showing him "where to line up [and] which waves to go for" (Coleman 2004, 199). As a competitive surfer, Aikau reached several finals of the Duke Kahanamoku Classic before winning the contest in 1977. Aikau finished 12th in the inaugural year of the Association of Surfing Professionals world tour ("Men's Events Champions" undated).

The Aikau family was part of the Hawai'ian cultural renaissance in the 1970s, a cause to which Eddie would ultimately give his life. As a part of this cultural revitalization, the Polynesian Voyaging Society built a full-scale replica of a *wa'a kaulua,* a double-hulled voyaging canoe, to demonstrate that Polynesian ancestors had explored, discovered, and settled Oceania from the west rather than passively drifting across the Pacific from the east. Launched in 1975, the *Hōkūle'a* commenced its second re-enactment of the 2,400-mile midocean crossing between Hawai'i and Tahiti in 1978, leaving Honolulu on March 16. The 16-member crew included Eddie Aikau. Five hours into the trip, the starboard hull began leaking and the *Hōkūle'a* listed and capsized, leaving the crew hanging on to the hull. The following morning, Aikau took a life vest, a rain slicker, a knife, and a strobe light and set out on a 10-foot surfboard for Lāna'i Island, 12 miles to the east. About 10 hours later the coast guard rescued the crew of the *Hōkūle'a,* but a weeklong search failed to find Aikau (Warshaw 2004, 8).

Aikau's biographer, Stuart Holmes Coleman, speculates on Eddie's death:

> Though he was a strong surfer, he probably didn't make much progress through the Moloka'i Channel. With the high winds and deadly currents being funneled between the islands of O'ahu and Moloka'i, it's one of the most dangerous channels in the world. Paddling against the currents would have been like trying to go upstream in a whitewater raft. By that evening, he had been without sleep for almost two days and nearing exhaustion. The 35 mph winds would have blinded him with saltwater spray, as the 10–12 foot waves washed over him. Sharks probably surrounded him as he clung to his board. (Coleman 2004, 224)

A commemorative plaque honors Aikau at Waimea Bay near the lifeguard tower where he worked.

In 1984 Eddie Rothman, a founder of Da Hui and a representative of the Aikau family, approached Bob McKnight, CEO of Quiksilver USA, with a proposal to hold a contest honoring Eddie (Jarratt 2006, 140). According to Rothman,

> Eddie was about two years older than me, and when I started surfing Waimea, he was the man. . . . He would see me paddling for a wave and he'd be like, "Go, bra, go!" or he'd go, "Yo! Let's go!" And we'd take off together. We became real good friends, and after he passed, every time I would paddle out at the Bay, I'd turn around to take a wave and hear his voice . . . "Yo! Let's go!" (Jarratt 2006, 141)

Rothman advocated "a simple affair, conducted over just one day, with no heavy commercial trips interfering with the intended spirituality of the occasion" (Jarratt 2006, 140). Seeing the contest as an opportunity to attach the Quiksilver brand to the "core of the Hawai'ian surf culture" (Jarratt 2006, 141) or, more realistically, to give the brand "the *appearance* of [cultural and historical] legitimacy" on the eve of its public listing on the New York stock exchange (Warshaw 2005/06, 91), McKnight embraced Rothman's proposal. Quiksilver subsequently sponsored the Eddie Aikau invitational surfing classic held in "middling, double-overhead waves at Sunset Beach in December 1984" (Jarratt 2006, 141). After that contest, which was won by Denton Miyamura, McKnight discussed its development with respected big-wave rider and contest director George Downing. Quiksilver subsequently moved the event to Waimea Bay and set out a new charter in which contests would be conducted only when the waves broke above 20 feet. The waiting period would be three months (December to February), and competitors would be elected to participate via a poll of peers (Jarratt 2006, 141–42). In Downing's words, "The Bay calls the day" ("The Quiksilver" 2008). Waimea has "called" surfers seven times between 1986 and 2009:

- 1987 (winner: Clyde Aikau)
- 1990 (winner: Keone Downing)
- 1999 (winner: Noah Johnson)
- 2001 (winner: Ross Clarke-Jones)
- 2002 (winner: Kelly Slater)
- 2004 (winner: Bruce Irons)
- 2009 (winner: Greg Long)

ancient hawai'ian chant   "Our guardian ancestors, there you stand behind us, there you stand in front of us, o guardians standing on the right, the voice in the heavens, the voice in the highest of highs, we greet you..."

Read by Kahu Butch Kauihimalaihe Helemano upon the announcement that the 2009/10 Eddie Aikau memorial contest would proceed ("Two Days at the Bay" 2010, 2).

Winning the Eddie Aikau Memorial in huge surf at Waimea Bay requires paddling power, extreme fitness, keen wave selection, the right equipment, and supreme confidence and courage. Eddie's younger brother Clyde won the contest in 1987, riding one of Eddie's boards, in 20-foot surf with an onshore wind. Clyde later described "Eddie's spirit rising to meet him in the lineup in the form of a large turtle surfacing just before the winning rides" ("The Quiksilver" 2008).

A low-key Keone Downing, son of George Downing, won in 1990 under the event's new moniker, "Eddie Would Go." Keone had been surfing Waimea since 1973 and, according to Ricky Grigg, was "always one of the best" (Jenkins 1999, 167). Keone refused to confirm reports that he embarked on an intense training program for the contest, saying only that "I was completely focused. Nothing distracted [me]. That can be difficult in big waves, but I didn't let anything in—the elements, the games your mind wants to play. I didn't even *see* the other people." At the end of the contest, he simply said, "I surfed in the memory of Eddie Aikau" (Jenkins 1999, 176).

Preliminary rounds of "the Eddie" were staged in 1995, but the swell disappeared before the contest could be concluded and didn't return during the designated waiting period.

Huge surf battered Waimea in 1998 and, ironically, not even the shrine of big-wave surfing could handle the swell. Competitors watched 30-foot-plus waves for several hours on January 28 before Downing canceled the contest. Among the competitors in the preliminary rounds in 1995 was Noah Johnson. He began tow-in surfing two years later and was a noted performer during the big swell of January 1998. The following year he defeated some of the biggest names in big-wave surfing to win the Eddie.

Ross Clarke-Jones, an invitee to every Eddie, and a perennial favorite to win the contest, finally achieved his dream in 2001:

My devotion to this event has been total for the past 12 years. I've
wanted it so hard and for so long that I think I've put too much pressure on myself and my past performances have been a bit disap-
pointing. To win has been a dream for so long that I had almost
given up on it. It's not even the money. I've spent 10 times that
amount just staying here every winter waiting for the event to happen. It's purely the prestige. To be able to say you've won The
Eddie. (Faen 2001)

The last three winners have been Kelly Slater (2002), Bruce Irons (2004),
and Greg Long (2009). The victory is "awesome, I can't really describe
the feeling," said Slater, the then 6-time world surfing champion (now 10).
"I can't really compare it to anything. It's just in a separate category . . . because it happens so rarely. It stands alone" (Lee 2002).

Irons and Long both won competing in their first Eddie Aikau contests
and in thundering surf with 40-foot wave faces. Both scored perfect 100-
point rides. Irons's score came on a 35-foot monster that commenced with
a critical take-off and concluded in a death-defying closeout tube in the
shorebreak ("The Quiksilver" 2008). The face of Long's wave exceeded
40 feet; he "survived a nearly sheer drop" before the wave "exploded at

Kelly Slater may have won 10 world championships, but he cemented his
credentials as an extreme surfer only by winning the Eddie Aikau Memorial contest
in 2002 (*above*) and placing second in 2009. *Source:* AP Photo/Ronen Zilbermen.

[his] heels and a towering wall of whitewater swept over him like a horizontal avalanche" (Thomas 2009). The performances of Irons and Long embodied the essence of the competition and captured the enduring memory of Eddie Aikau, the man who would always go.

laird hamilton (1964–)

A professional surfer, stuntman, model, renowned waterman, and highly respected big-wave rider, along with Buzzy Kerbox and Darrick Doerner, Laird (Scottish for "lord") Hamilton pioneered tow-in surfing in the early 1990s. In August 2000 he successfully rode a slab of unfathomable power at Teahupo'o. The ride won Hamilton the Action Sport Feat of the Year at the ESPN Action Sports Awards. Surf journalist Sam George says, "If you measure Laird by any standard, he's the greatest living surfer in the world today. No one can touch him as far as performance, innovation, imagination, pure athleticism, and just absolutely unquestionable courage" (*Step into Liquid* 2003, ch. 4). "Over the past 20 years," says Ben Marcus (2009, 102), Hamilton has "pushed surfing higher, faster, deeper and in more strange directions than anyone else."

Born Laird Zerfas in San Francisco, Laird arrived on the North Shore of Oʻahu with his mother, JoAnn Zerfas, in 1967 shortly after the breakdown of her marriage. Playing in the shorebreak at Pupukea, the four-year-old Laird became entangled with legendary surfer Billy Hamilton. Back on the beach, Laird looked him in the eye and, according to Billy, said, "I want you to be my Daddy. So you have to meet my mommy. Come meet her" (Jenkins 1997, 87). Laird confirms the story: "I chose Bill. He was Superman to me. Superman's my father, and I'm gonna do everything just like him" (Jenkins 1997, 87). Billy and JoAnn married shortly after, and Laird took the Hamilton surname.

From a very early age, Hamilton's notion of fun meant risking his body. At the age of five he attached one end of a rope to a slab of building tile that he buried, and the other end to his waist. He then threw himself into the raging shorebreak at Pipeline where the lateral current was running around 20 knots. At 8 years old he leaped 60 feet from the famous Waimea dive rock; at 13 he surfed 12-foot waves at Hanalei; his first bungee jump was a 700-foot leap from a bridge in Sacramento; and he rode his first street luge head-first—his face traveling at 60 miles an hour mere inches from the concrete track.

In 1992 Buzzy Kerbox persuaded Hamilton to try tow-in surfing behind the former's motorized inflatable boat. Initially the pair experimented at Backyards, near Sunset Beach. At the suggestion of Gerry Lopez, they transferred the experiment the following year to the north coast of Maui and Jaws. There the waves break at 20 feet perhaps a half-dozen times a year and, occasionally, at twice that size. In the Jaws laboratory Hamilton and a coterie of friends, known as the "Strapped Crew," developed tow-in surfing; they replaced inflatable boats with personal watercraft, designed and manufactured specialized boards with straps for the feet, and practiced teamwork and safety drills (*Strapped* 2002). In this extreme environment Hamilton effectively took command of the activity and within a few years established a reputation as the world's tow-in expert and leading big-wave rider.

Hamilton cemented his status on August 17, 2000, at Teahupo'o when Darrick Doerner towed him into what many consider the meanest wave ever tackled, a slab with a 20-foot face and a lip half as thick. Journalist Michael Fordham describes the wave rather like Jack London might:

> [A] figure appears in the line of sight. Laird Hamilton drops the tow rope. The rail and the fins of Laird's board dig into the wave's face. As he angles, his right [back] leg begins to bend more and more, and his left [front] straightens as the surface he is attempting to ride becomes steeper and the transfer of kinetic energy becomes increasingly extreme. [I]t looks as if he is the point of stillness in a vortex, then, as if he is travelling backwards, the wave begins to arch and to detonate on the reef.... Then Laird is gone, sucked deep into an explosion of mist as the huge tube spits. [A] moment later the rider of the beast emerges—arms wide, shooting out of the mist at speed and flying on to the shoulder to safety. (Fordham 2008, 232; see *Riding Giants* 2004, ch. 27, 01:25:57–01:26:17; *Laird* 2001, ch. 6, 26:20–26:35)

The intensity of the experience brought tears to Hamilton's eyes, and the surfing world marveled over his incredible ride. The following quotes, in the surf documentary *Riding Giants* (2004, ch. 28), capture the awe-striking footage:

- Matt Warshaw: "It's the single heaviest thing I've seen in surfing. What could be heavier than that?"
- Sam George: "The most amazing, single most significant ride in surfing history. It completely restructured...our entire

perception of what was possible. Laird had to drag his back hand, on the opposite side of his board, to keep himself from getting sucked up in that hydraulic. In the middle of that maelstrom, how did his mind say, 'this is what I have to do?' No one had ever ridden on that wave as Laird rode. It was the imagination of dealing with that unimaginable energy and coming up with the plan, spontaneously."

- Steve Pezman: "When that photo came out, it stopped everyone's heart."
- Greg Noll: "Man, that shit's impossible. You don't do that."
- Pat Curren: "In my absolute prime there was absolutely no way I could ride a wave like that."

Hamilton abhors official, organized surfing competitions, something he attributes to watching his stepfather get "burned" in controversial contests and to what he considers is a system that manipulates young people: "How do you judge art?" he scoffs. Thus Hamilton shies away from big-wave competitions such as the Tow-in World Cup, the Big-Wave Challenge, and the XXL Big Wave Awards. Hamilton also does not brag about his achievements: "you'll never hear from me, 'I rode the biggest wave'" (Duane 2004). Such boasting, he argues, merely establishes a "benchmark

On August 17, 2000, Darrick Doerner towed Laird Hamilton into a wave at Teahupo'o that many consider the meanest ever ridden. *Source:* Tim McKenna.

that people want to step over" and ultimately undermines one's credibility. Hamilton insists that success is much more than a single performance on one big wave; rather it is "about your body of work." Yet, Hamilton clearly understands that in the quest for social prestige he must be seen and that he cannot totally remove himself from his peers. In the late 1980s and early 1990s, for example, Hamilton spent several seasons at Pipeline establishing his credentials:

> At that point in my life, I needed to find out if I could surf at that level. I needed to surf Pipe just like everyone else did. And I had local guys giving me shit. So I had to go through the line up, each guy, and have a confrontation. Fortunately for me—and them—I didn't have to go to brawls. A lot of people understood how serious I was. (Jenkins 1997, 103)

Today, Hamilton's views about competition and publicity seem more grounded in marketing strategy than principle. As Daniel Duane (2004) comments, "by staying above the fray, surfing only for himself, he has become a lone, untouchable Neptune, reigning over a swelling pantheon of competing demigods." Indeed, Hamilton artfully employs the media to enhance his profile and status. Among his media appearances Hamilton can count correspondent for the syndicated cable series *The Extremists,* host of the Fox Sports Network's *Planet Extreme Championships,* surfing as a stunt double for Pierce Brosnan in the James Bond adventure *Die Another Day,* screen time in the surf documentary *Step into Liquid* (2003), and leading role and production credits in the Sony Pictures big-wave-riding documentary *Riding Giants* (2004). More recently Hamilton has started his own company, BamMan Productions, in which he is the

---

watermen   Among the most proficient extreme surfers are a small group who are skilled in multiple oceanic pastimes such as diving, fishing, paddling, swimming, and wind surfing, as well as being highly knowledgeable about the ocean and the weather. Known as watermen, these surfers, such as Brian Keaulana and Laird Hamilton, pursue one mission: "to wrestle with the forces of the Ocean, to become one with it, in as many ways are humanly possible" (Carroll 2009, 108).

star performer, producer, and owner of every second of Laird water-action footage.

In 1990 Hamilton and Kerbox paddled the Molokai Channel, between Oʻahu and Molokai (30 miles), the English Channel (23 miles), and from Corsica (France) to Elba (Italy) (44 miles) (Diamond 2006, 101–8). In the late 1990s Hamilton began experimenting with tandem boards as equipment with potential to teach his children to surf. His experimenting included the incorporation of a paddle. Hamilton was actually rediscovering a traditional practice in Hawaiʻi that merged canoeing and surfing, and was reintroduced by the beach boys of Waikiki in the 1960s who used canoe paddles to move their surfboards around the breaks. "Beachboy-style surfing," says Waikiki figure Bobby Achoy, began "out of laziness; it enabled them to remain high and dry while taking snapshots of tourists—and also kept their cigarettes dry" (Bradley 2007). Hamilton quickly became addicted to it, designing new equipment that gave birth to the standup paddleboard (SUP) (Weir 2008). Hamilton's *Laird* SUP (12'1" long, 31" wide, 4.13" thick), produced by Surftech, entered the market in 2004 and helped popularize the boards. In June 2006 Hamilton spent an arduous six hours crossing the English Channel on a SUP:

> I started on stormy and rough conditions [and there was] a lot of traffic [with] ships coming from every direction. I met a big storm in the middle of the crossing and that slowed me down as…I faced front winds. The last [two and a half miles] were the most difficult because the current was against me and I was tired and it felt like I was paddling in place. ("Peddle and Paddle" 2006)

Hamilton believes SUPs will revolutionize surfing; they offer surfing the same opportunity to diversify as cross-country skis offer skiing, he says (Krantz 2008, 2B). The diversity of SUP surfing especially appeals to Hamilton: "I went down the Colorado River, I've been across the English Channel, all the channels in Hawaiʻi, [I] ride giant waves, ride small waves; it's like a dance." He aims sometime to paddle the Bering Strait and paddle through a hurricane (Weir 2008).

Hamilton's detractors criticize his ego and maniacal attitude. Yet, tellingly, they speak publicly only on condition of anonymity. On the other hand, Hamilton's supporters shower him with the highest praise. "Laird," says fellow waterman Brian Keaulana, "is like every single element known to man. Raw power that the ocean has. Strong foundations of mother earth.

He can be as calm as the sea, as strong and swift as the wind" (Jenkins 1997, 120).

What are the qualities of a legendary extreme surfer? Looking back on the big-wave riders who ruled the North Shore of O'ahu in the 1950s and '60s, Ricky Grigg (1998, 37) observes that they all possessed a "rugged individualism" and a "complete comfort with themselves." They "did things their way" and were "strong, sometimes stubborn, unique, unconcerned with group values, often alone but never lonely." In addition, Grigg continues, they "were all-around watermen—swimmers, divers, paddlers, sailors." However, as I have suggested, perhaps the overriding traits are courage and prowess in extreme conditions. These traits, which involve mental as well as physical capability, translate into the power to command others to "go," even against their instincts.

6. technicalities

The whole method of surf-riding and surf-fighting, I learned, is one of non-resistance. Dodge the blow that is struck at you. Dive through the water that is trying to slap you in the face. Sink down, feet first, deep under the surface, and let the big smoker that is trying to smash you go far overhead. Never be rigid. Relax. Yield yourself to the waters that are ripping and tearing at you. When the undertow catches you and drags you seaward along the bottom, don't struggle against it. If you do, you are liable to be drowned, for it is stronger than you. Yield yourself to that undertow. Swim with it, not against it, and you will find the pressure removed. And, swimming with it, fooling it so that it does not hold you, swim upward at the same time. It will be no trouble at all to reach the surface.

Jack London (1911, 77–78)

in constant flux and motion, the ocean is a dynamic environment, which makes surfing a highly technical affair. Surfers quickly learn that currents can transport them into the take-off zone and that rips provide shelter from closeout sets. Confronted by partially collapsing mountains of water, surfers instinctively paddle toward an unbroken section or, if staring at a pitching lip, they know to "slip" under the concentrated power. Surfers understand that they must take extra-deep breaths before being submerged by wave energy. Surfers realize they should dive deep to escape the turmoil of a breaking wave. When they wipe out in extreme surf, surfers curl their bodies into a ball. Maverick's regular Grant Washburn likens a big wave to "a wrestler": "Once he's got your arms, you can't get them back. It's like tearing a chicken wing off" (Thomas 2008). Professional surfer Nathan Hedge knows the feeling. Falling and landing on what he described as "concrete" at Teahupo'o in the final of a contest in 2004, Hedge's outstretched left arm hyperextended behind his body and came out of its shoulder socket. "I remember trying to get up but I only had one arm to use. Thank God it wasn't that big and I got out of trouble pretty easy, although at the time it was pretty dramatic and tragic" (*Blackwater* 2005, ch. 11). Surfers learn to stroke smoothly and efficiently to catch waves, to angle their boards down the face, to guide their boards up and down the wall, and to cut back to stay with the power of the break. In this chapter I examine the more technical aspects of extreme paddle-in and tow-in surfing. I group the discussions into three themes: equipment, training, and rescues.

equipment

Paddling-in to big waves requires a specially shaped big board, which surfers call a "gun," short for "elephant gun": "You can't shoot elephants with a BB rifle," Buzzy Trent once famously declared. "You need an elephant gun" (Warshaw 2000, 35). As I noted in chapter 2, the face of a breaking wave mimics a treadmill, with the speed of the water drawing up the wall increasing as it becomes more vertical. At some point this water will push even the strongest paddler on the most buoyant board behind the crest. A standard gun today is shaped like a cross between a needle and a teardrop: 9 feet 6 inches long, 20.5 inches wide, and 3.13 inches thick, with a pronounced rocker, or curve through the board (particularly at the front) and a pin-shaped tail (Fordham 2008, 223).

The leg rope, or leash, is controversial equipment in big surf. Laird Hamilton considers the leg rope the single most dangerous thing involved when surfing waves over 20 feet. In big surf, leg ropes prevent surfers from diving deep to escape the energy of the wave and white-water turbulence; in wipeouts they can wrap around the surfer's neck, drag the surfer over "the falls" with the board, or "tie" the surfer to an underwater reef. At Maverick's, Darryl "Flea" Virostko's leg rope became entangled with a rock and held him in place while eight successive waves battered him. Virostko struggled to release his leg rope, likening the fight against the powerful current to "doing a sit-up with 200 pounds on your chest" (*Riding Giants* 2004, ch. 16). In another incident at Maverick's, Jeff Clark's leg rope hooked him to a large "sail" rock after he was hurled into the "boneyards"—a collection of jagged rocks:

I can't get the leash off my ankle, and this broken half of my board is dragging me right into the rocks. Finally, I'm getting swirled around, and I got my hands out, and I feel the rock. And I'm hanging on to the side of this rock, and I'm under water, and the water starts to drain, and I'm high and dry. The next thing you know, another wave came over the rock and I'm under water again; the tension from my legrope relieved, and I climbed on top of the rock and I got rid of that damn anchor. (*Riding Giants* 2004, ch. 16; Beck 1993, 15)

One theory blames Mark Foo's death at Maverick's on his leg rope tying him to the bottom (Warshaw 1995a, 102). (Footage of Foo's last wave shows him hitting the water, skipping along the surface and being thrown over the falls [*Extreme Surfing* 2000, ch. 4].) When Mike Parsons wiped out on the wave after Foo, he too was held down by an entangled leg rope—that eventually snapped—and during his time underwater Parsons felt a body slam into him. At first, Parsons thought the body was Brock Little, who wiped out beside him. But film of the wave showed Little had already surfaced and that his body could not have been the one that struck Parsons (*Riding Giants* 2004, ch. 17; *Extreme Surfing* 2000, ch. 4). On the other hand, leg ropes can, under certain conditions, provide a lifeline, a means by which disorientated surfers can haul themselves back to the surface—and air.

The "big guns for big waves" motto influenced pioneer tow-in surfers. On one of their first expeditions, in 15- to 20-foot waves at Laniakea, Laird Hamilton, Burton "Buzzy" Kerbox, and Darrick Doerner rode a 10-foot balsawood gun, which they agreed "felt solid" (Lopez 1995, 94). However, just as paddle-in surfboards progressively shortened, so too did tow-in boards. Hamilton's instincts finally persuaded him that shorter boards would be faster and, with straps "gluing" them to their boards, riders would be able to slice through surface chop (Lopez 1995, 94). During his first session at Jaws, Hamilton rode a 7-foot-10-inch board 16 inches wide with three layers of 6-ounce fiberglass on the bottom and six layers on the top (Lopez 1995, 94). Hamilton continued to shorten his tow-in boards. Today, he rides boards that are 6 feet 2½ inches long, 16 inches wide, and between 1½ and 1¾ inches thick, made of solid wood (balsa with a spruce stringer) and weighing 15 to 22 pounds. Wood, Hamilton says, has greater "absorption power" than a heavily glassed light foam blank and offers more "core weight" and strength. Hamilton has built heavy foam boards with multiple stringers that "almost" mimic wood, but he inevitably returns to the latter: "My three favorite boards are balsa wood," he says (Bass 2004a).

Hamilton maintains that the weight of the board is critical to performance, especially in windy and choppy conditions. Here he draws the analogy of "a light car on a bumpy road":

> You drive down a really bumpy road with a really light car at a high speed and the car is just bouncing all over the place. You get a big old Cadillac [that] weighs four-thousand pounds and you drive down a bumpy road and you barely feel it. The tires might be vibrating under the car but the car is not jumping around. (Bass 2004a)

As well as adding weight to deal with chop (produced by direct winds and refractions off cliffs and mountains, personal watercraft [PWC], and boils on the face), Hamilton shapes his boards to "make 'em forgiving": a good board will have "nose kick" and "soft rails up front" to help deaden the impact of the board hitting the wall or the bottom of the face on the take-off (Bass 2004a). Lastly, Hamilton emphasizes the importance of fins on tow-in boards: "We're going a lot faster, so we're more sensitive to fin design. The faster you go the less fin you need, but the better foiled it needs to be." "Ultimately," Hamilton believes, "it would be nice to get rid of the fins completely... because that would be the least amount of drag. That's why boogie boards go so fast, the less fin you have the faster you go. The faster you go, the less fin you need" (Bass 2004a).

Towing-in required surfers to learn new skills, especially with respect to depositing riders on the right wave, in the right place, at the right time. Initially, drivers used the so-called windsurfing method, whereby they tracked the wave and then led the rider down the face, remaining in front for the duration of the ride. But this technique generates chop on the wall which presents obstacles for the rider. Today, drivers generally tow from behind the peak and "kick" the PWC over the top of the swell/crest. This method also allows the rider to maintain tension in the tow rope and for the driver to "whip" his or her partner into the face at maximum speed. An even more advanced technique involves the driver accelerating toward the front of the wave, turning before the face, and whipping the rider onto the wall. Using this technique a rider can enter the wave at speeds of 50 miles an hour (*Billabong Odyssey* 2003, ch. 5).

Regardless of the method, drivers need impeccable timing. Depositing riders too early can leave them without a wall and possibly stranded in the impact zone of successive waves; holding riders too long can leave them "behind the peak" and "too far back to make the wave" (Lopez 1995,

---

footstraps   While riding a wave, surfers maneuver their boards by shifting their weight and pressing with their heels or pressing with their toes. Footstraps, a key development in tow-in surfing, give riders better leverage. With footstraps, riders have stronger control over the board because they can exert force upward as well as downward—for instance, they can actively lift with their toes while they press with their heels. But in a wipeout, footstraps can lock the rider to the board and increase the risk of injury (Hamilton 2008, 217).

101–2). Veteran North Shore lifeguard and president of Hawai'ian Water Patrol, Terry Ahue insists that driving a PWC requires a lot of experience. Drivers need to know "when to run" and where to exit; they must be able to time sets and, above all, they need a "cool head" (Jenkins 1993, 55). Even the best can err. When his longtime surfing partner Brett Lickle towed Laird Hamilton into one wave at Egypt, a few miles west of Jaws, the tow and release proceeded smoothly, but Hamilton entered the wave a shade high on its face. "Brett and I did everything right," insisted Hamilton, "but sometimes, in the ocean, being right isn't enough." Hamilton bailed, jumping out the back of the wave to escape the crush of water (Brent 2008).

PWC introduced a "long and intimidating" list of hazards to surfing, observes journalist Bruce Jenkins (1993, 52 and 55). Just getting a PWC in and out of a shorebreak is like dealing with "an 800-pound bowling ball" which could easily kill someone (*Billabong Odyssey* 2003, ch. 8). In the surf, PWC can become deadly projectiles. After towing his partner, Raimana Van Bastolaer, into a 10-foot wave at Teahupo'o in May 2005, Reef McIntosh maintained his focus on the surfer rather than the wave, which "caught" the 800-pound PWC as it began to break. The lip under which Van Bastolaer was gliding now contained a PWC, which flew just inches past the surfer's head. "You realise how fast things can go wrong and what you should and shouldn't be doing," a shaken McIntosh mused later that day. Van Bastolaer, who saw the PWC from the corner of his eye, was especially gracious: "We lost the ski, but good thing we never lost my friend and myself, so it's ok" (Doherty 2008, 35th moment).

Once under the power of the ocean's forces, anything can become a hazard including boards and sleds (which can weigh over 50 pounds).

After Hamilton bailed at Egypt (see above), he bobbed in the ocean waiting for Brett Lickle to collect him. Lickle arrived on the scene quickly,
and the instant Hamilton was on the sled he sped to safety. But the wave
was too quick and engulfed them; three other waves followed. Eventually,
Hamilton and Lickle were carried out of the impact zone but Lickle was
badly hurt: a fin from a spare board had "flayed open his left leg from the
back of the knee to the ankle":

> Blood gushed from the wound, clouding the water and causing Ham-
> ilton to fear that the fin had punctured Lickle's femoral artery. They
> were half a mile offshore, and no other surfers were in sight. Hamil-
> ton realized there would be no help—it was all on him. He stripped
> off his wet suit and cinched it above Lickle's wound. He swam in a
> dead sprint to the [PWC], afraid that, behind him, Lickle was bleed-
> ing to death or, potentially even worse, that the blood spurting into
> the ocean would serve as chum for the tiger sharks that cruise the
> reef....
>
> The [PWC] engine started. Its radiophone still functioned. Stark
> naked and reeling from the quarter-mile sprint and his own beating

Deadly wipeout: In extreme wipeouts the surfer is at the mercy of the elements
and rogue equipment. Kyle Davidson, The Island (New Zealand), 2004. *Source:*
Mark Stevenson.

by the waves, Hamilton radioed 911 as he raced to pick up Lickle. The sharks hadn't discovered him. Hamilton screamed into shore, steering with one arm, cradling his hemorrhaging friend with the other. An ambulance met the surfers on the beach. Lickle's femoral artery was intact, but the wound would require 53 staples to close. (Brent 2008; see also Casey 2010, ch. 10)

Even the seemingly innocuous towrope can be a hazard. One time, Michael Willis was waiting in the impact zone at Jaws for his partner to snatch him from the face of a monster when the PWC stalled. Somehow, the towrope, which was drifting in the water, wrapped around Willis's right leg. The wave crashed over the driver and Willis and dragged the latter, now attached to the ski, some 400 yards. As the wave dragged Willis and the PWC, the rope progressively tightened and cut deeper into his leg muscle. Willis was extremely lucky; the injury confined him to crutches for just two weeks (Carroll 1997, 24).

training

Surfing requires quick reflexes, balance, power, speed, and endurance; peak oxygen-uptake levels in surfers compare favorably with "those reported for other upper-body endurance-based athletes" (Mendez-Villanueva and Bishop 2005, 55). While the popular perception of extreme surfers is that they are daredevils, big-wave riders such as Ken Bradshaw dismiss such labels. Bradshaw considers extreme surfers "risk technicians": "We understand the risks we're facing; we understand what we have to do to get out of these situations that we put ourselves in" (*Extreme Surfing* 2000, ch. 2). Indeed, the biographies of extreme surfers all draw attention to meticulous preparation and rigorous training. Jay Moriarty may be remembered as the 16-year-old who endured the wipeout of the millennium at Maverick's in 1994. However, he had successfully ridden the break numerous times before that day and, moreover, had trained and prepared himself under the auspices of Maverick's elder Rick "Frosty" Hesson for two years before he caught his first wave in 15- to 18-foot surf late in the winter of 1993/94. Training and preparation were Moriarty's life insurance policies.

As well as a physical training program based on running, swimming, and cycling, Hesson encouraged Moriarty to analyze his surfing techniques, training schedules, and contest performances; he encouraged him to visualize riding Maverick's including minute details about sun, wind,

---

james michael "jay" moriarty (june 16, 1978–june 15, 2001) Renowned for his positive attitude toward life, Moriarty, a Maverick's regular and accomplished competitive longboarder, died the day before his 23rd birthday near the Lohifushi Island resort in the Maldives. While practicing breath control in deep water, he lost consciousness and drowned (Borte 2001).

---

surface conditions, and bad scenarios. "I wanted Jay to vanquish panic, 'the broker of survival,'" said Hesson. He forced Jay to always keep five alternative plans of escape at the forefront of his mind. Within six months Moriarty proved to Hesson that he was serious. He had "built himself into a well-conditioned athlete and had prepared himself mentally for any nasty eventuality Maverick's might throw at him." After his headline-grabbing wipeout, Moriarty spoke to Hesson by phone: "What you taught me saved my life. If you hadn't helped me train and practice all those things, I would have died" (Smith 1996, 104–9).

The modern training regimes of the leading extreme surfers are a long way from the approaches adopted by the first generation of big-wave riders at Makaha. In the 1950s, although Buzzy Trent ran, skipped rope, and shadowboxed to develop and maintain fitness, during flat spells of surf most of his peers preferred to "lounge on the beach...phlegmatically working their way through several cases of Primo beer" (Warshaw 2000, 34). Laird Hamilton pursues two training regimes. In summer, when the big swells dissipate, his weekly program includes two hours of nonstop circuit training, with an emphasis on lunges, presses, squats, and powerlifts; 3 to 10 miles of stand up paddling; hill climbing on a mountain bike with 50 pounds strapped to the cycle; and running on the beach with a 100-pound log harnessed to his body. As well as improving lung capacity, those last three activities—cycling, running on sand, and standup-paddle surfing—help Hamilton build strength in his legs, which he insists is crucial: at Rincon (Southern California) "you catch four waves [and] at the end your legs [are] shaking" (Bass 2004a). During winter, the big-wave season on Maui, Hamilton spends less time in the gym and more time on the water or on his bike. Hamilton's challenge is "not to overtrain": "As I've gotten older, I've become more systematic. I pay attention to cycles and seasons. You can't play the Super Bowl every day" (Brent 2008).

Diet is also important in Hamilton's training. While he concedes "it's harder to eat correctly and stay away from processed foods," Hamilton subscribes to the dictum "potato chips in is potato chips out":

> You eat potato chips, you're going to perform like a potato chip. It's just the rules. And if you're able to get away with it because you're that talented, you're still just deceiving yourself because in the end you're either going to have a short-lived career or you're just not going to be performing at the level that you could. So either way you're shortchanging yourself. But there is balance of course. You need to be able to enjoy certain things too. It doesn't mean you can't have coffee, but you need to have balance too. Everything in moderation. (Bass 2004a)

Training for wipeouts in big surf means preparing for hard impacts—impacts that Brian Keaulana likens to "being hit by a Mack truck"—and developing the lung capacity and relaxation skills to deal with long submersions in turbulent water. Keaulana's training regime for increased lung capacity includes diving to the ocean bottom, then picking up rocks and running along the ocean floor (*Extreme Surfing* 2000, ch. 2); for stamina he recommends paddling—hundreds of miles—in open waters (*Extreme Surfing* 2000, ch. 3). Cheyne Horan suggests that surfers can begin "serious breathing and breath-holding techniques and methods" by going underwater "breathing out for 20 seconds so that there is nothing in your lungs, and then holding it for a further 20 seconds." Then "you've got to ... hold for 50 [seconds]." Of course, Horan adds,

> just 'coz you can hold your breath for a long time doesn't mean you'll be alright. Sometimes you surface in a wipe-out situation, and there's another massive wave bearing down on you. So to simulate this, you've got to hold for 50, swim to the surface, then go straight down for another 50 seconds. If you can pull this off 4 times you'll be alright... you're simulating a 4-wave set. If you can deal with it you'll be in a good place. What happens when you do it all the time is that you start recognising the moment, the exact time that your body is hurting for air. Then after a while you start relaxing with that moment. This is when you're starting to deal with the situation. (Horan undated)

Hamilton reinforces the importance of such relaxation when he notes that "holding your breath for 30 seconds when your heart is hammering 200

Placing a rider on the right wave, in the right place, at the right time requires practice and training. Tane Tokona depositing Oscar Smith, The Island (New Zealand), 2008. *Source:* Mark Stevenson.

beats a minute is like holding it for 5 minutes when you're sitting in a chair" (Brent 2008).

Along with Hamilton, Darrick Doerner and Dave Kalama emphasize the importance of mental fitness and the close relationship between "physical health and strong mental health" (Bass 2004a). "The human body can withstand a lot of pressure," says Doerner, reflecting on an incident in which he was caught inside by "the biggest thing I'd ever seen" at Moving Mountains (Kahana Valley, Oʻahu) in 1994. "When you're mentally not there, you're physically not there," he declares. "You have to have a positive attitude about big waves...otherwise you'll perish" (Wolf 2000, 26–27). Kalama attributes much of his ability to "confidence," which he insists is "a state of mind...an attitude." Importantly, confidence does not come "instantly," rather, "you have to earn it,...build it, and...go through all the processes" (*Extreme Surfing* 2000, ch. 3).

How long are the careers of big-wave surfers? "People keep asking me, 'how long can you keep taking the poundings, Ken?' I don't know," admits Ken Bradshaw, although at age 49 he believed he would "try for another ten years" (*Billabong Odyssey* 2003, ch. 13). Buzzy Trent remembers the day he decided to retire:

I was thirty something when I last paddled out and I said to myself, "This is the last wave I ride. This is the way I want to go out." I went all the way to the Point [Makaha], caught a *beautiful* wave, paddled into the beach and that was it. I never rode again. Sold my board, quit, completely cold turkey. For me it had to be that way. (Moniz 1990, 49)

Deeming "instinct...every bit as important as judgment," Peter Cole believed that he "lost the capability to ride the largest waves" as he aged because "I think too much": "The crowd sitting inside detracts from my concentration so that I have lost the natural instinct to take off. I back off more than I ride" (Brady 1983, 42).

Interestingly, Hamilton conceptualizes his career "following two lines on a graph":

One line shows my physical systems, stuff like VO2 max and fast-twitch muscle fibers, either flattening or very gradually declining. The other line shows the intangibles—maturity, experience, judgment, passion, perspective—steadily rising. The two lines cross at an interesting place, and I regard that place as my peak. It's not a point, but a plateau. Your peak isn't really a product of your body, but of your enthusiasm. (Brent 2008)

Research into human physiology supports Hamilton. In men, muscle mass, balance, flexibility, heart function, and maximum oxygen uptake peak at around 30 years old and then begin to slowly decline. Heart rate decreases 6 to 10 beats per minute per decade, thigh muscles start to lose density, intramuscular fat increases, and the number of type-2 (fast-twitch) muscle fibers decreases. Lung function and capacity, anabolic hormone levels, and the number and quality of neural pathways also show inexorable declines. VO2 max (sometimes written VO_{2max}), which measures maximum cardiovascular performance, decreases around 10 percent each decade. Through hard training and determination, athletes can maintain peak endurance and performance for around five years and slow the rate of decrease until around 50 when the pace of decline quickens under the weight of lower lactate threshold, lower exercise economy, and lower VO2 max. However, researchers have been unable to identify the precise physiological mechanisms by which VO2 max declines over time, leaving them to postulate that decreases in performance are more closely associated with "reductions in exercise training intensity," that is, "reductions in energy, time, and motivation to train." In other words, the performances of older

---

ten-time world champion kelly slater on aging

"I think I can get a lot better, actually. I watched Tom Carroll retire from the tour at like 29–30 years old; and I was baffled because at 35 and even 40 I saw him surfing at what I thought was better than when he was winning world titles in the '80s. I definitely took that on board. It's absurd to think that physical age is any kind of indicator of what you can do. I feel like that in ten years time [in my mid-forties] I can still be in the running for winning contests. It's really what you do with your mind and your body to keep you in the right space" (Slater 2008).

---

athletes decline because they taper their training, pay less attention to nutrition, and succumb to injury—usually under psychological, emotional, and social pressures that lie outside their sporting milieu. One positive conclusion from these findings is that if surfers, like Hamilton, aim for "consistently high-quality performances, rather than peak performances," then they can perhaps extend their careers for many years (Brent 2008).

Yet, although surfers may be able to extend their performances at some level, this does not necessarily translate into maintaining their place in the fratriarchy. After a long career at Waimea, Fred Van Dyke became afraid to go. Realizing that he no longer belonged at the shrine, Van Dyke decided to limit himself to waves under 10 feet. His decision cost him friends:

> None of them would admit it, but I wasn't one of the big-wave gang anymore. It bothered me. It hurt. I was like the castrated cat in the neighborhood; all the other cats beat up on you because they know something's different. (Warshaw 2000, 187)

rescues

Modern surfing developed as an individual pursuit in which each surfer took responsibility for his or her self. In the early years, boards were rudimentary and there were no leg ropes, flotation devices, or lifeguards to rescue surfers. At some breaks, the question of rescuing surfers from the impact zone in big surf was not even considered, let alone attempted.

During his heat in the Eddie Aikau memorial contest at Waimea Bay in 1987, Brian Keaulana lost his board after wiping out on a 20-foot wave and was swept into the impact zone for a merciless beating: "I would get held under by one or two waves and as I came up and grabbed a quick breath there would be another one crashing down on me." Keaulana did not expect anyone to rescue him: that "would have been suicide" ("The Launch" 1993). Of course, individuals tend to "vanish" in big swells, obscured by waves and spray. During one large swell which closed Sunset Beach, Buzzy Kerbox and Laird Hamilton took the opportunity to tow-in. They were under the impression that Darrick Doerner was watching them from the lifeguard tower on the beach. But when they later asked Doerner for his thoughts, he merely asked, "about what?" Most times "nobody's gonna be watching" extreme surfing, says Doerner, adding that if "something goes wrong out there, you don't come home" (Jenkins 1993, 55).

In the remainder of this section, I present a fivefold typology of rescues in big surf: self-rescues, help from other boardriders, advice from the shore, PWC, and helicopters.

Self-rescues: In most cases, surfers venturing into big waves must rely on their own skills and knowledge to ensure their safety. The most basic, and essential, skill is swimming. Surfers have to be able to swim long distances if they are separated from their boards. Doerner recommends anyone entering the extreme-surfing realm be able to swim five miles (Jenkins 1993, 50). Some surfers strap fins to their waists in case they are separated from their craft and have to swim miles to shore. Ken Bradshaw once hitched a ride to Outside Leftovers with Terry Ahue where the waves were breaking around 25 feet. Bradshaw lost his board and Ahue couldn't find him. Ahue returned to Waimea Bay where he found Bradshaw sitting in the lineup; he had swum back to the beach, picked up another board, and paddled back out (Jenkins 1993, 52).

Safety also depends on knowing the break—the lineups, dead water, impact zones, rips. When Ken Bradshaw lost his board to a 30-foot closeout set at Waimea and the "rip pulled him into the danger zone," he knew precisely what he had to do. He swam, says Mark Foo, "all the way into the lineup and tried to stroke it in again; but again the rip pulled him toward the killer shorebreak and again Ken had to swim back out and around. It took two full cycles before he made it to safety. It was an impressive display of water knowledge and stamina" (Foo 1985, 69).

Help from other boardriders: Most surfers will, of course, assist peers in trouble, if it is possible. In many cases such assistance is life saving.

After his surfboard hit him in the chest in 20-foot surf at Sunset Beach in October 1995, leaving him with a punctured lung and several broken ribs, Ross Clarke-Jones struggled for breath and was on the verge of lapsing into shock. Clarke-Jones was lucky: his rescuers were experienced big-wave riders Darrick Doerner, Charlie Walker, and Mark Foo. Confronting a powerful west swell closing out the main break at Sunset and with short lulls between sets, Doerner and Walker decided to tow Clarke-Jones north to look for a channel where they could bring him ashore safely. It took them nearly 45 minutes to reach a channel between Velzyland and Back-yards (Wolf 2000, 5–6).

Advice from the shore: Sometimes assistance comes from another set of eyes on the shore. After Jeff Clark, as mentioned in the previous section, overcame the problem with his leg rope to climb on to the "sail" rock in the boneyards of Maverick's, he now had another problem—getting ashore:

> A massive wall of white water came roaring in. I lay down ... and held on while the wave rolled over me. I realized that I was going to be here for a while. [T]he current would suck all the water out from around the rocks during the sets, leaving nothing to swim in to get out of there. The chance of me swimming back out through the white water was not a good option. There were also cracks that I could wedge my right arm and knees into. I just held on for wave after wave. I knew my longevity would be severely limited if I got hy-pothermia or fatigued my muscles to such an extent that they were useless. I started shaking and moving my arms to get the circulation going between waves.

Clark's savior, Jim, was close at hand, having scrambled to the top of a 15-foot-high rock about 25 feet away:

> He asked ... if I needed a helicopter. I told him I was ok. For the next half hour, Jim kept me informed as to when to brace myself for a big swell and when to get up and rest for a moment. Jim shouted, "Look out!" An unusually large inside wave ... bur[ied] me with several feet of water. Within seconds, Jim shouted, "Jeff, jump now!" I didn't hes-itate. I trusted Jim's judgement as I knew he'd be conservative in a situation like this. I swam the 30 or so yards of swirling, boiling white water to the edge of the tidal flat just as another set started to roll in. (Beck 1993, 15)

Clark walked out of the water.

PWC: Personal watercraft not only facilitated tow-in surfing, they revolutionized surf rescues. After surviving his thrashing at Waimea Bay during the Eddie Aikau memorial contest in 1987, Brian Keaulana investigated the possibility of using PWC as rescue equipment. He bought a Yamaha WaveRunner and suggested to fellow lifeguard Terry Ahue that they "figure out how to use these things to make rescues" ("The Launch" 1993). Co-opting other big-wave surfers and lifeguards, including Melvin Puu and Dennis Gouveia, Keaulana and Ahue researched and developed the equipment and techniques for PWC rescues and later formed Hawaiian Water Patrol, which became the preeminent extreme-surf-safety service. Hawaiian Water Patrol developed the sled, a large bodyboard that attaches to the back of PWC and which can accommodate multiple patients ("The Launch" 1993).

PWC introduced the notion of teamwork rescues. Indeed, such are the conditions and circumstances on some days at some breaks that a partner willing to commit to rescues is a prerequisite for surfing. At Jaws, for example, the energy of the wave runs all the way to the cliff, and surfers who fall have "issues," says Mike Parsons: "They have to get rescued; there is no way of getting out of there on your own" (*Making the Call* 2003, ch. 4). Because contemporary tow-in techniques leave the driver behind the crest of the wave and unable to see the rider (see above), the "Strapped Crew" positioned a PWC in the channel as an added safety feature (*Strapped* 2002). Keaulana, however, is wary of relying on machines. He believes that surfers should depend on themselves: "If you put yourself in heavy situations you'd better make sure you can get out of it without a machine" (*Billabong Odyssey* 2003, ch. 1).

Helicopters: In big seas, helicopters are also used to undertake rescues. When he wiped out at Third Reef Pipeline in 20-foot surf, Curt Carlsmith may have considered it a stroke of luck that a helicopter pilot, filming Robbie Nash windsurfing at Phantoms, saw the wipeout and flew in to pick him up. When the chopper arrived, Carlsmith grabbed the helicopter's landing skids. Yet as this story demonstrates, timing is often critical in such rescues. While maneuvering into position, the pilot had failed to notice an oncoming wave about to break on the chopper. By the time he realized the impending danger, he had to take immediate action; he lifted away with such velocity that Carlsmith lost his grip on the skids and fell from a considerable height into the water. Tragically, Carlsmith landed

Safety is paramount in extreme surf, and partners rely on each other to provide assistance. Anthony Walker tracking Llewellyn Thomas, The Island (New Zealand), 2007. *Source:* Mark Stevenson.

on the water head and shoulder first. The impact severed an artery, and Carlsmith bled to death (Wolf 2000, 41).

Rescues by helicopter tend to be public events, and, not surprisingly, given their desire for waterman status, many big-wave surfers prefer to avoid such scenes. When a helicopter arrived to pluck Mark Foo from tumultuous seas at Waimea Bay on January 18, 1985, he waved it away. Although he had just been hit by a monstrous wave that closed out the entire bay, Foo believed he could still catch a smaller 20-footer to shore. However, large waves continued to roll through the bay, each imprisoning Foo underwater for extended periods and preventing him from returning to the take-off zone for the desired wave. Despite the conditions, he waved the helicopter away a second time. Effectively washed out to sea, Foo found himself confronting the biggest set of the day. On the second wave, he turned and took the drop, falling some 25 feet. When Foo finally surfaced, the helicopter pilot was there again offering his services; this time Foo gratefully accepted (Wolf 2000, 38–39). Recounting the incident, Foo explained:

> I waved [the rescue helicopter] off because I still figured I could ride one in. [The wave I chose] backed off momentarily, long enough to take off and start driving. Then, again, the whole thing started

sucking and turning concave. I kept it all together as I free fell ver-
tically a good twenty-five feet on my board. But the flight was too
long and the wave too concave and I crashed upon contact with the
wave face. I hit so hard I saw stars, then I started bouncing down
the face.... I felt the explosion of the lip; I heard my [board] snap; I
felt my watch break away from my wrist and then felt myself getting
sucked up and over for another thrashing. Things turned pretty grey.
(Foo 1985, 70 and 88)

Surfers undoubtedly gain much pleasure from riding monstrous waves,
but their pleasure ultimately depends on their training, preparations, and
skill, while their survival often requires assistance from others. In short,
big-wave surfing is highly technical and, as we shall see in the concluding chapter, becoming more so as surfers continue to search for bigger and
steeper waves and to push themselves deeper into the barrel.

7.   futures

I was resolved that on the morrow I'd come in standing up....[T]o-morrow, ah, to-morrow, I shall be out in that wonderful water, and I shall come in standing up....And if I fail to-morrow, I shall do it the next day, or the next. Upon one thing I am resolved...I, too, [will] wing my heels with the swift-ness of the sea, and become a...Mercury.

Jack London (1911, 79–80)

ancient polynesians well knew the pleasures of surfing, the joy and thrills of sliding down and gliding across breaking waves. Calvinist-inspired missionaries, determined to eradicate any expression of cor-poreal pleasure, tried to ban surfing in the early and mid-19th century. (Elsewhere their brethren banned a wide range of popular amusements.) Later that century, Victorian middle classes, with their Christian mores, sanctioned codified sports—regimented, disciplined, time-bound, and spatially demarcated games. Although surfing persisted during the ban (Moser 2008), it did recede in Hawai'i and only reemerged in the early 20th century as a popular pastime under the auspices of the burgeoning tourist industry, which sanctioned the fundamental human drive for plea-sure and which afforded surfing space to develop. As a tourist writer Jack London discovered the delights of surfing; his enthusiastic and enrap-tured words helped spread the pleasures of the pastime abroad. Surfing diffused around the globe during the 20th century, repeatedly facilitated by technological advances, especially increasingly lighter and maneuver-able boards that made the sport more accessible and more pleasurable.

Today, surfing rides a growth trajectory, fueled in large part by a new philosophy of physicality which, ironically, celebrates corporeal pleasure and rejects those 19th-century values initially responsible for prohibitions on the activity and then the codification of sports. Popularly labeled extreme, this new philosophy emphasizes individuals rather than teams. Individuals seeking personal challenges and competing against themselves lie at the heart of extreme sports, in contrast to the team as the embodiment of a collective identity (communities, provinces, states, nations) seeking to symbolically defeat opponents. In extreme sports, victory means completing an exceptional maneuver or achieving an extraordinary experience. Unlike mainstream sports, where the athlete performs on artificial and formally designated spaces (e.g., courts, arenas, fields, ovals, tracks, pistes) at formally recognized times (e.g., start, finish), extreme sports blur the boundaries between the body and the environment. Extreme sports typically involve an interaction with the earth's natural forces—gravity, wind, waves; indeed, survival frequently depends on an intimate knowledge of these forces, which can change suddenly. While some devotees conceptualize their involvement in extreme sports in terms of conquering the environment (e.g., a mountain, a set of rapids, a wave), more often they attach spiritual and religious personas to the earth's forces and stress harmonious relationships with Mother Nature (Brymer, Downey, and Gray 2009; Kotler 2006; Poirier 2003). Surfing pioneer Tom Blake viewed nature as "synonymous with God: for a brief period of the ride, [the surfer shares] God-given energy.... One might say surfriding is prayer of a high order, that the sea is a beautiful church, the wave a silent sermon" (Blake 2000, 11). This harmony can also extend into equipment. Nick Ford and David Brown (2006, 162), for example, refer to the surfboard as a "hybrid extension of the body."

Extreme sports provide ideological and practical alternatives to mainstream sports and their values (Rinehart 2000, 506). Participants in the former often cultivate "outlaw" images and convey general attitudes of irreverence. Social irreverence has long been a hallmark of surfing. Whereas professional athletes in mainstream sports tend to conceptualize sport as work, participants in extreme sports view sport as "part of their lifestyle" and fun (Rinehart 2003, 32). "I just turned 37 and I've never had a real job and I'm pretty proud of that," says "Camel," one of the "Magnificent Seven" profiled by *Tracks* in its "Outlaw Issue" (November 2009). Living on unemployment benefits, the West Australian surfer says he's "never been sponsored but I've had a lot of waves." One reason Camel fears employment is that it would mean "losing touch with the ocean," "the one thing I'm definitely in tune with," he adds in a Dora-esque tone (Kennedy 2009b, 46).

Pleasure is the essence of extreme surfing. Oscar Smith, The Island (New Zealand), 2008. *Source:* Mark Stevenson.

In his own way Camel identifies pleasure as the essence of surfing. The pleasure may be fleeting, says Maverick's regular Mark Renneker, but "for those time-warped seconds, life is pure. There is no confusion, anxiety, hot or cold, and no pain; only joy" (Warshaw 2000, 201).

If pleasure is the essence of surfing, then the ocean and its waves are the source. In concluding this book I return to waves as the subject that ultimately frames all discussions about surfing, including its future. Here I discuss the wave through four interconnected themes: crowding, the rideable realm, forecasting, and artificial reefs.

crowding

Surfers ride only an infinitesimal fraction of the waves that break on any one day, yet crowding is a fundamental issue and source of discontent, especially at quality sites bordering metropolises and at popular surfari destinations. (Oceanographer James Walker [1974, 79–94] offers an interesting scientific discussion of crowding and the capacity of surf breaks that takes into account a range of factors such as physical dimensions of the break, number of riders on the wave, number of rideable waves per unit of time, length of ride, rate of wipeouts, time to return to the take-off zone, and riding style of the surfers.) Around 5,000 surfers descend on the North Shore of Oʻahu in mid-winter, including professionals, aspiring professionals, locals, and members of the surfing media and industry. Although the 25 miles of coast between Kaʻena and Kahuku points contains approximately 50 breaks, on an average day only 12 to 25 are working, with perhaps as few as four firing. Walker (1974, 94) uses the term "suppressed" to describe surfing as a sport. By this he means that the demand exceeds the opportunities to catch waves. Not surprisingly, "violence and mayhem hang in the air like seaspray" (Warshaw 2000, 146). At Malibu good surf regularly draws 100 surfers to a break that cannot support 50. Under this pressure the water "dissolves into chaos," with "all the established rules...flying out the window. Surfers scramble for any piece of energy they can get, dropping-in on others, colliding, getting in each other's way" (Marcus 2008, 31). Such are the pleasures of sliding down and gliding across perfect waves at these breaks, and others like them, that some surfers erupt in violent fury at the mere thought of another rider interfering or disrupting their thrill. On the periphery of a heaving crowd at a perfect Jeffreys Bay, surfer and journalist Craig Jarvis waited patiently for his turn. Eventually he "snagged...a choice nugget" and rode the longest wave he had ever seen. At the end Jarvis felt "exhilarated" and "high from the rush." Reflecting on the euphoria Jarvis (2009, 90) admitted that "if someone had dropped-in on me and ruined it for me, I surely would have fought that person. I would have tried to hit that person in the face with my fist, over and over again, whether they hit me back or not."

Jarvis's candidness exposes the innate egoism of the human species and the nature of testosterone-charged crowds at surf breaks. It also challenges Peter Singer, Professor of Bioethics at Princeton, who believes surfers could be taught to share waves and to gain vicarious pleasure from watching and assisting others (Baker 2007, 238–45).

Crowding played a causal role in the global diffusion of surfing. It encouraged surfers to search for "undiscovered" breaks (ironically, exposing them to more riders) and to experiment with tow-in surfing. Crowds drove Buzzy Kerbox to use his Zodiac motorboat to tow-in Laird Hamilton on the North Shore of Oʻahu in 1991: "To ride waves without anyone else around, that was what got the whole thing started for me" (Warshaw 2004, 321).

Tow-in surfing should, in theory, dissipate crowds and open the ocean playground, but in practice it has remained a minority pastime pursued largely by devotees of extreme. After the discovery of Todos Santos, Mike

Parsons anticipated it would quickly become overcrowded. But the surfers "drawn by the hype" tended to be the ones who were "worked over" by the waves and "now, almost ten years later, you go out there on a big day and it's pretty much the same crew" (Long 1999, 107). Some surfers compound crowding by using personal watercraft (PWC) in small surf at popular paddle-in breaks. Longtime Waialua (Oʻahu) surfer, and president of the North Shore Ocean Safety Association, Michael McNulty complains about drivers "towing surfers in to 3-foot surf," and he echoes the sentiments of thousands of paddle-in surfers when he says that towing-in should be "strictly for big waves" (Toth 2003).

Laird Hamilton also criticizes tow-in surfers who violate traditional paddle-in breaks. "The etiquette of surfing," says Hamilton, affords "the lesser vehicle...right of way. You don't take your motorbike down to a bike path." In his view, tow-in surfers "should go somewhere else or just don't go [in the water] until [paddle-in surfers] are gone" (Bass 2004b). On the other hand, Hamilton also recognizes that there will be times when even the mildest break is unsuited to paddling and that towing is the only option. Under these conditions, paddle-in surfers should not attempt to exclude others: "that's where the other side's not playing fair" (Bass 2004b). Hamilton identifies this as something of a problem at Maverick's where some surfers paddle out and "sit on the shoulder [to] make a point":

> OK, well great, congratulations but you're not catching anything. Maybe you're catching one little end shoulder bowl but...you're not being productive and you're not really taking advantage of the opportunity. OK, yeah you caught a shoulder on one, but then you missed the last 10, no one got them and everybody could be getting all there is to offer. It's like eating part of a dinner and then throwing the rest of it away. (Bass 2004b)

Responding to complaints and safety concerns, states and local councils around the world have passed laws restricting PWC operations in the near shore and demarcating specific areas for launching; many have also introduced testing and licensing for drivers (Toth 2003). While certification and licensing requirements irritate some tow-in surfers, others believe they will help improve safety and remind surfers of their responsibilities. "This way there's less people in the water who don't know what they're doing," says Charlie Clifton, a tow-in surfer: "There are too many people out there getting in the way and causing trouble, making a bad name for the people who've been towing-in for a long time and know the water. It's like getting a license to drive," he adds, and will "make things safer" (Toth 2003).

the rideable realm

Hamilton believes that surfing means "any form of riding a wave" (Bass 2004a). He rejects narrow definitions of the activity and believes that surfing will continue to expand in the future particularly as surfers reconceptualize the realm of the rideable. Tow-in surfing reconceptualized the notion of a rideable wave with extreme surfers increasingly tackling slabs of ocean that break on reefs and rocks with little, and occasionally no, water over them. Indicators (northwest Western Australia), for example, is "an extremely heavy ledging and twisting wave" that "breaks just metres away from the rocks in front of the Bluff." Kerby Brown considers Indicators "the most dangerous set-up" he has seen. The wave

> comes marching out of really deep water and just explodes. You basically have to ride next to the barrel on the first section as the lip lands on dry rock and then you have no choice but to go and backdoor the boils and ledges while hoping it doesn't go completely dry before it spits you out into the channel. ("Dry Water" 2009, 128)

At the other end of the spectrum is the open ocean swell, which recently has been made available to surfers with an innovation called the foilboard.

The foilboard—developed by Laird Hamilton—consists of a board connected via a strut or an arm to a foil that sits under the water and rides the energy of the wave below the surface. Although the foil is underwater, the board rises out of the water and thus avoids chop on the surface and ensures a smooth ride. Hamilton likens the foil to an underwater aircraft that the surfer effectively "flies":

> You're standing on this board but you're really standing on a plane. You're flying the plane by leaning forward, the plane dives; lean back; lean right, the plane turns right; lean left; and then everything in between. (Bass 2004a)

Foilboards will allow surfers to "break the planning hold barrier and go to the next dimension," which is "faster" and "free from the effects of surface conditions" (*Laird* 2001, ch. 7) and they will enable surfers to ride under and through the water—a third dimension (Bass 2004a). Moreover, foil-boards don't rely on breaking waves and will open ocean swells to surfing (*Laird* 2001, ch. 7) and in theory allow surfers to ride a swell for hundreds of miles (*Billabong Odyssey* 2003, ch. 12). Nonetheless, whether foil-boards progress beyond their current novelty status remains to be seen.

Hamilton also dislikes discussions around categoric definitions of waves, or landmark events such as the mythical 100-foot wave. While Hamilton wants to ride the biggest waves, he argues that quantifying them is narrow and risks reducing the pastime to "one climactic moment." "I have a hard time knowing how big it is half the time. . . . We just go, 'hey it's big today' or 'today it's friendly' or 'today it's not friendly' or 'it's shallow here' or 'this is a thick one'" (Bass 2004b). As Hamilton asks, what happens after the 100-foot wave? Does that mean "you're done? You stop? That would be sad." (Bass 2004b).

Yet, for all the reconceptualizations of waves over the last 20 years, extreme paddle-in surfing remains the gold standard. Towing might provide access to an abundance of colossal waves, but there are costs, including the loss of the drop and the destruction of serenity. "I just love the feeling of paddling-in and grabbing your rail and scooping up under the lip into

Paddling-in to a long wall and dropping down a steep face remains the gold standard of extreme surfing. Craig Baxter (*left*) and Doug Young (*right*), Papatowai, 2006. *Source:* Mark Stevenson.

the tube" at Teahupo'o, says Laurie Towner. "For me that's [a] twenty-times better feeling than being towed-in early. Towing just isn't the hardest thing in the world to do" (Webber 2009, 51). "The thing about tow surfing," says Garrett McNamara, a dual winner of the Tow-in World Cup at Jaws, is that "an 80-year old, water skiing grandma could grab the rope and catch the 100-foot wave. She might not make it, but... anyone can do it" (Slater 2007, 121).

When Rusty Long talks of perfection he refers to a 12- to 15-foot session at Todos Santos in February 2007: "It was just a serene big-wave surf. No one else there. No PWC riff-raff... it just allowed you to enjoy a few drops and appreciate your surroundings. The colors were unlike anywhere else in the world" (Slater 2007, 118). Maverick's regular Mark Renneker believes towing destroys the delicate balance of paddle-in surfing that Matt Warshaw (2000, 201) calls "equipoise": "Air, water, wind and swell; energy stored and expelled; the ninety-nine parts anticipation against one part release; the slow, metered pulse of a trans-Pacific swell against the apocalyptic flash of a huge breaking wave."

It seems, however, that surfboard technology will always impose limits on the type of wave surfers ride as well as how they ride. "Normal surfboards are one-dimensional," says Hamilton, and "their surface area dictates the angles of what [can be done]. You [can] turn and go on an edge or another edge and maybe you can pop and air and get off the water," but it's essentially confined to one plane (Bass 2004a). This is unlikely to change in paddle-in surfing. In answer to the question "What Will Surfing Look Like in 20 Years?" *Waves* magazine warned readers not to expect much change in surfboard design. "It would be awesome," *Waves* wrote, "to anticipate a truly innovative plan-shape but it ain't likely. The safe bet is that the decade will again be shaped by trends, modifications and left field rediscoveries" ("What Will Surfing" 2009, 82).

forecasting

Traditionally, "predicting the size of the waves arriving on the coast" was regarded as "one notch up on the difficulty scale from predicting the weather" (Butt, Russell, and Grigg 2004, 7). In spite of the challenges of the task, wave forecasters have achieved remarkably accurate and fine predictions. As Todd Chesser prepared to paddle to Outside Alligators on February 13, 1997, a member of the civil defense approached and advised him against entering the water, warning that a large swell was due to hit the coast around 11:00 A.M. Considering the warning but not heeding the direction to stay out of the water, shortly before 11:00 A.M. Chesser and two peers agreed they would paddle out farther as a precaution. They were too late. At 11:00 A.M., on cue, the horizon darkened and the swell marched in. The three surfers "drove through the face of the first wave." Chesser stood on his board from which he dived deep to avoid the second wave; he repeated this action on the third wave, which broke from top to bottom almost directly on him. Chesser's body was found shortly after, floating face down in the impact zone (Marcus 1997, 54).

The new horizon in scientific wave forecasting lies in the area of advance predictions. Currently, scientists base their calculations on information from land- and sea-based sources (e.g., wave buoys, weather stations) that enable forecasters to identify quality surf a week in advance. Meteorologist, surf forecaster, and director of Swellnet.com, Ben Matson believes that information gleaned from satellites, which provide more frequent data, will become increasingly incorporated into wave forecasting and will "make it easier to classify swell[s] . . . before they reach the coast." Matson foresees ongoing advances in "the accuracy of the weather models used to underpin surf forecasts." Yet, he does not believe these will eradicate the "degrees of error extending out past four or five days." In short, surfers will not "suddenly have pin-point accuracy at three weeks' [notice]" ("What Will Surfing" 2009, 84).

Most big-wave breaks are still notoriously fickle and hard to predict. The mid-ocean Cortes Bank, for example, is highly exposed to the elements and can only be ridden in less than 10-knot winds and with the swell coming from one direction. According to Sean Collins, such conditions may align on as few as five days a year, and then of course you have to *be* there. Collins monitored Cortes Bank for 10 years before he successfully predicted a good day (*Step into Liquid* 2003, ch. 21).

artificial reefs

Crowding at popular surf breaks also raises speculation about increasing the supply of perfect waves—creating another Kirra, Rincon, Jeffreys Bay, Raglan (New Zealand), Pipeline, or Trestles (Southern California)—by constructing artificial reefs that give shape to disorganized swell. Interestingly, many iconic waves are the products of human intrusion: Superbank (Queensland) in Australia, and Sandspit (Santa Barbara), Harbormouth (Santa Cruz), and Wedge (Newport) in California (Butt 2009).

Scientists and engineers have been predicting a brave new world of artificial reefs since at least the mid-1960s (LaTourrette 2005, 13). Kerry Black, a former managing director of ASR, believes the debate over the technical feasibility of artificial reefs has abated: "It's been really well accepted.... The issue of whether they work is now a bit out of date" (LaTourrette 2005, 14). Indeed, artificial reefs are producing results. Cables (Perth), for example, produces an average of 142 rideable days per year at a site that previously produced less than half this number (Borrero 2008). But when Black adds "I think" to the end of his sentence about popular acceptance of the technical achievements, it is clear there is ongoing debate.

Jose Borrero (2008) insists the science is robust and has "created good surfing waves"; he believes "reef type projects have never been given a fair chance in terms of budgets or expectations relative to 'traditional' coastal engineering projects." In contrast, Chad Nelsen, an environmentalist with the Surfrider Foundation, a non-profit organization dedicated to protecting oceans, waves, and beaches for recreation and enjoyment, challenges scientists' claims that they can design artificial reefs to produce quality waves:

> The naïve enthusiasm of the average surfer, including the average surfer scientist, results in this incredibly optimistic view. People get so excited about these things that they lose sight of the fact that the jury's still out—only [four] of these things [Narrowneck, Gold Coast; Mt. Maunganui, New Zealand; Cables; Pratte's Reef, California] have been built in the world. (LaTourrette 2005, 14)

Failed artificial reefs, such as Pratte's (El Segundo, California), illustrate the debate. A "tiny budget" and placement "too close to the shore" "doomed" the reef, insists Borrero (2008). However, Nelsen says the real lesson from Pratte's is that the basic structure of reefs on which waves break is more complex and can be double the vertical elevation of what they first appear (LaTourrette 2005, 14). Leslie Ewing, a coastal engineer with the California Coastal Commission, concurs. She insists that the construction of artificial reefs for high-quality surfing waves "will continue to be an art for a long time." "The science," Ewing says, will not produce a reef with "all the attributes of a natural break" (LaTourrette 2005, 15; see also Warshaw 2010, 470–73).

Certainly the argument that artificial reefs will reduce crowds does not bear close scrutiny. In California, for example, an estimated 1 million surfers share around 5,000 breaks; in raw numbers this means around 200 surfers per break. Adding 1,000 reefs might theoretically reduce the number of surfers per break to 170. But the complex psychology of crowds and resources suggests that in practice a successful, quality reef is more likely to *increase* crowds. Nelsen uses a freeway analogy to explain the psychology:

> By building new lanes on freeways what you do is take a lot of people who might be otherwise taking the bus, and they're like "oh cool, I can drive now," so you're actually increasing the number of cars. [I]t's the same thing with crowded surfing areas and new surf spots. (LaTourrette 2005, 17)

Nelsen's argument is even more persuasive considering that some local councils (e.g., Bournemouth, England; and Tauranga [Mt. Maunganui], New Zealand) conceptualize artificial reefs as a way to attract tourists (i.e., crowds). Indeed, after surfing a sizable swell at Cables, local Matt Szwedzicki described the experience as "average and crowded," while local Chris Sheenan declared that the construction at Narrowneck had "created a circus in the water" (Sanders 2005).

Artificial reefs also raise philosophical issues around development, the intrusion of humans into the natural environment, and disruption of the natural ecology (Butt 2009).

---

extreme pollution Contamination of the ocean by fertilizers, heavy metals, oil, pesticides, and sewage destroys marine ecologies and makes surfing impossible. The disastrous three-month long oil spill in the Gulf of Mexico in 2010 (April–July) is one example. In the case of oil, there have been few advances in technology over the last two decades to decontaminate oceans and shorelines (Fountain 2010). Evidence from previous disasters reveals that attempts to remove oil from beaches "can cause as much, if not more damage" and that ongoing clean-up operations tend to delay the recovery of ecosystems (Butt 2009, 122).

While there are as many opinions and viewpoints on these issues as there are surfers, it is worth reflecting that, by definition, "extreme" in sports implies dealing with the unpredictable forces of nature. Modifying those forces means changing the connotations of extreme. In the case of extreme surfing it would also mean changing the essence of "go," a fundamental notion that refers to the command surfers issue to their peers as they mentally weigh up the risks of extreme take-offs and is a metaphor for demonstrations of courage in dangerous surf. "Go" has shaped modern big-wave riding since surfers dared venture to Makaha in the early 1950s.

glossary

aloha.   (a) A salutatory term for "hello" and "goodbye" in Hawai'ian. (b) A philosophy of grace and generosity toward others.

backdoor.   A maneuver in which the surfer approaches the barreling peak of a wave from behind and makes the ride by tucking into the wall and under the pitching **lip.**

barrel.   See **tube.**

bowl.   A concave, bowl-shaped face of a wave, usually associated with a shallower marine topography that bends the wave shoreward and causes it to break suddenly and with more force.

caught inside.   A surfer caught inside is trapped between the shore and an approaching set of waves. The severity of the situation depends on the power and intensity of the surf. Most surfers are caught inside following a **wipeout** or by **rogue waves.**

charger.   A hyped-up, over-enthused surfer who takes-off on any wave, irrespective of its dimensions and with total disregard for his or her own safety. See also **fratriarchy.**

closeout.   A wave that breaks along its entire length leaving no wall for the surfer to traverse/ride.

crest.   The highest portion of the wave before it breaks.

deep inside.   See **inside.**

drop.   The initial slide down the face of the wave after **taking-off.** See also **late drop.**

drop-in.   Stealing the inside priority to a wave or, more dangerously, joining a wave being ridden by another surfer.

feathering.   Plumes of spray blowing off a peaking wave before it begins to break.

feralism.   An extreme form of surfari in which the traveling surfer camps at remote surf locations for extended periods and lives a subsistence existence.

fratriarchy.   A hierarchical brotherhood whose members pursue and accrue status and prestige through physical prowess, which in surfing means **charging** the biggest, most ferocious waves.

grommet.   A young surfer with intense enthusiasm for the pastime.

groundswell.   Waves that approach the coast in long parallel lines and are typically caused by distant storms.

hold down.   A situation in which the force of a breaking wave "holds" a surfer under water. Most hold downs follow a **wipeout** or occur when the surfer is trapped in an **impact zone.** A strong hold down may last 5 seconds, an extreme form 20 seconds. While seemingly brief, hold downs are accompanied by violent, energy-depleting forces that sap the body of oxygen. Hold downs often occur in succession, and typically leave the surfer furiously struggling for air.

impact zone.   The area immediately in front of the breaking wave; the zone where the wave breaks with maximum force.

inside.   (a) The portion of the **wall** closest to the foam. (b) The surfer closest to the **peak** holds the inside position and the right to the wave. (c) A surfer under the **lip** or in the **tube** is said to be deep inside. See also **caught inside.**

kook.   A derogatory term for beginning surfers whose inexperience and demeanor brands them in the surf and on land.

late drop (aka late take-off).   **Taking-off** as the wave is breaking. This maneuver usually places the rider in contact with the **lip.**

left break, lefthander (abbrev. left).   A left-breaking wave, the curl of which breaks from right to left as defined from the vantage point of a surfer in the water and facing the shore (e.g., Pipeline, Teahupo'o).

lip.   The pitching tip of a hollow wave.

localism.   The territorial defense of a surfing locale. Locals claim priority over the waves on the grounds that they live nearby or regularly surf the break. At some breaks—for example, Palos Verdes, Pipeline, and Ours (Sydney)—intense localism can lead to violence against non-locals.

ocean swell. See **swell.**

outside. Seaward from the area where most waves in the set break.

over the falls. A type of **wipeout** in which the surfer becomes entangled in the **lip** of the breaking wave and carried "over the falls." The power of the water in the **lip** may drive the surfer into the water below and, if that water is shallow, into the ocean floor/sandbar/reef underneath.

paddle-in surfing. Most surfers catch waves by lying prone on their surfboards and paddling hard, using an alternating arm stroke. On big waves over 30-feet surfers cannot generate enough speed by paddling to **take-off.** See also **tow-in surfing.**

peak. The highest point of the advancing wave, where it first begins to break; the peak usually provides the **take-off** zone at a surf break.

pit. The bottom of a hollow wave, between the foam and the shoulder of the wall. See also **trough.**

right break, righthander (abbrev. right). A right-breaking wave, the curl of which breaks from left to right as defined from the vantage point of a surfer in the water and facing the shore (e.g., Maverick's, Waimea).

rogue waves. (a) Any unexpectedly large wave during a session. (b) Extreme storm waves that reach heights 2.5 times greater than the highest one third of waves in a given storm.

section. A portion of **wall,** usually 30–45 feet or more, that breaks as one block. A tricky section may be difficult to ride (e.g., exceptionally steep or fast breaking), or it may break in front of the rider.

set. A group of usually three to seven waves that arrives at a break during a **swell.** Sets of waves typically arrive at regular intervals ranging from a few minutes to 30 minutes or more.

shoulder. The unbroken portion of the wave next to the peak that marks the beginning of the **wall.**

slab. A wave that takes on the appearance of a huge slab of ocean without a back. Slabs typically crash like concrete onto the reef.

swell.   (a) All the waves generated by a particular storm (e.g., the swell of 1969). (b) An unbroken wave in open ocean generated by a storm (c.f. **windswell**).

swell window.   The direction (usually noted as a range of compass degrees) from which a wave-producing depression will produce the best surfing conditions for a particular site.

take-off.   Catching a wave. In competitive surfing, judges deem the rider to have caught a wave when, in the process of standing up, the rider's hands leave the rails (sides) of the board. See also **late drop.**

tow-in surfing.   A more recent form of surfing in which the driver of a personal watercraft tows the rider into waves that are typically too steep, too big, or breaking too fast for the surfer to access by the more traditional means of paddling-in. In tow-in surfing the rider avoids the pitfalls of the **take-off.** See **paddle-in surfing.**

trough.   (a) The lowest point between two crests in an ocean swell. (b) The very bottom portion of the wave before it breaks. See also **pit.**

tube.   A type of breaking wave in which the crest pitches out and away from the advancing wall to form a barrel or hollow tube.

wall.   The unbroken face of a wave; the part of the wave that surfers spend most of their time riding. See also **peak** and **shoulder.**

windswell.   Typically small and uneven waves caused by local onshore winds.

wipeout.   When a surfer falls off the surfboard. The severity of a wipeout depends on the type of wave being ridden and the location on the wave where the surfer falls. In powerful, hollow waves, a surfer may fall on the face, fail to penetrate the surface, and be sucked upward into the **lip,** which then throws them **over the falls.**

bibliography

Abraham, P. 1999. "Paradise or Bust." *Deep,* Summer: 42–57.

Abrams, M. 2009. "Being Maya Gabeira." *ESPN Surfing,* August 27. http://espn.go.com/action/news/story?page=Maya%20Gabeira.

Arnett, R. 2006. "Tiger's Antics in New Zealand Should Be Questioned." *SportsIllustrated.com,* April 25. http://sportsillustrated.cnn.com/2006/writers/rick_arnett/04/25/tiger/index.html.

"Australia's Fifty Most Influential Surfers." 1992. *Australia's Surfing Life* 50: 70–123.

Baker, T. 2007. *High Surf.* Sydney: HarperSports.

Barkow, J. 1975. "Prestige and Culture: A Biosocial Interpretation." *Current Anthropology* 16 (4): 553–72.

Barilotti, S. 2002. "The 10 Most Powerful Waves on Earth: Fact, Folklore, Fatalities." *Tracks,* November: 20–36.

Barnes, B. 1995. *The Elements of Social Theory.* London: University College of London Press.

Bass, S. 2004a. "Laird Hamilton: Part One." *Surfermag.com online.* http://www.surfermag.com/features/onlineexclusives/lairdintrvu/.

Bass, S. 2004b. "Laird Hamilton: Part Two." *Surfermag.com online.* http://www.surfermag.com/features/onlineexclusives/laird_prttow/.

Bartholomew, W. 1976. "Bustin' Down the Door." *Surfer,* December 1976/January 1977: 74–82.

Bartholomew, W. 1996. *Bustin' Down the Door.* Sydney: HarperSports.

Beck, L. 1993. "Man Imitates Abalone." *Surfer's Journal,* Winter: 12–15.

"Biggest Cortes Bank Surf Ever Challenged Spark Excitement for Billabong XXL Big Wave Awards" 2008. *Surfline,* January 8. http://www.surfline.

com/surf-news/press-release/biggest-cortes-bank-surf-ever-challenged-spark-excitement-for-billabong-xxl-big-wave-awards_13085/.

Billabong Odyssey. 2003. Prod. Vincent Leone and Dir. Philip Boston, 87 minutes, Arenaplex, DVD.

Bird, E. 2000. *Coastal Geomorphology: An Introduction.* Chichester, UK: Wiley.

Blackwater: The Story of a Place Called Teahupo'o. 2005. Prod. and Dir. Tim Bonython, 62 minutes, Globe, DVD.

Blake, T. 2000. "Voice of the Wave." *Australian Surfer's Journal* 3 (1): 11.

Booth, D. 2001a. *Australian Beach Cultures: The History of Sun, Sand and Surf.* London: Frank Cass.

Booth, D. 2001b. "From Bikinis to Boardshorts: *Wahines* and the Paradoxes of Surfing Culture." *Journal of Sport History* 28 (1): 3–23.

Borrero, J. 2008. "Pratte's Reef Redux." *Surfline,* November 12. http://www.surfline.com/surf-news/one-researchers-opinionit-didnt-have-to-end-like-that-prattes-reef-redux_20360/.

Borrero, J. 2009. Email correspondence between Jose Borrero, Felipe Pomar, and Ben Marcus, January 2008, forwarded to Douglas Booth by Jose Borrero, February 9.

Borte, J. 2001. "Jay Moriarty." *Surfline,* November. http://www.surfline.com/surfing-a-to-z/jay-moriarty-biography-and-photos_868/.

Bra Boys. 2006. Prod. and Dir. Sunny Abberton, 90 minutes, Garage Industries and Bradahood Productions, DVD.

Bradley, G. 2005. "Surf Sessions Show Off Sunny's Side of Life." *New Zealand Herald,* October 25, D13.

Bradley, T. 2007. "Stand Up and Paddle." *Around Hawaii,* August 1. http://www.aroundhawaii.com/sports/surf/2007–08_stand_up_and_paddle.html.

Brady, L. 1983. "Whatever Happened to Big Wave Surfing?" *Surfer* 24 (5): 40–49.

Brennan, J. 1994. *Duke: The Life Story of Duke Kahanamoku.* Honolulu: Ku Pa'a Publishing.

Brent, J. 2008. "Laird Hamilton: Ultra-Fit at 40." *Best Life,* May. http://www.bestlifeonline.com/cms/publish/fitness/The_Science_Riding_the_Storm.php.

Brown, W. 1993. "The Death of Dickie Cross." *Surfer,* October: 53 and 87.

Brymer, E., G. Downey, and T. Gray. 2009. "Extreme Sports as a Precursor to Environmental Sustainability." *Journal of Sport and Tourism* 14 (2/3): 193–204.

Bustin' Down the Door. 2008. Prod. Monika Gosh and Robert Traill, Dir. Jeremy Gosh, 95 minutes, Madman, DVD.

Butt, T. 2009. *The Surfer's Guide to Waves, Coasts and Climates.* Penzance, Cornwall, UK: Alison Hodge.

Butt, T., P. Russell, and R. Grigg. 2004. *Surf Science: An Introduction to Waves for Surfing.* Honolulu: University of Hawaii Press.

Caillois, R. 1958/2001. *Man, Play and Games.* Trans. M. Barash. Urbana, Ill.: University of Illinois Press.

Carroll, N. 1997. "Yikes!" *Good Weekend* (Supplement to the *Sydney Morning Herald*), December 6: 24–28.

Carroll, N. 2001. "The Price of Waves." *Surfline,* September 10. http://www.surfline.com/mag/pulse/2001/sep/09_10_price.cfm.

Carroll, N. 2009. "The New Waterman." In *The Surfing Yearbook,* presented by Surfersvillage, 107–9. Salt Lake City: Gibbs Smith.

Casey, S. 2010. *The Wave: In Pursuit of the Ocean's Greatest Furies.* London: Yellow Jersey.

Chase, L. 2008. *Surfing Women of the Waves.* Layton, Utah: Gibbs Smith.

Coleman, S. H. 2004. *Eddie Would Go: The Story of Eddie Aikau, Hawaiian Hero and Pioneer of Big Wave Surfing.* London: Yellow Jersey.

Conneeley, R. 1978. "Interview." *Tracks,* April: 15–19.

Cralle, T. 2001. *Surfin'ary: A Dictionary of Surfing Terms and Surfspeak.* 2nd ed. Berkeley, Calif.: Ten Speed Press.

Diamond, P., ed. 2006. *Surfing's Greatest Misadventures: Dropping In on the Unexpected.* Solana Beach, Calif.: Casagrande Press.

Doherty, S. 2005. "The Perfect Storm." *Tracks,* September: 22–36.

Doherty, S. 2008. *The Moment.* Sydney: Hachette.

Doherty, S., and B. Mondy. 2005. "The Kook." *Tracks,* September: 79–82.

Duane, D. 1998a. "Anatomy of a Big One." *Outside Magazine,* May. http://outside.away.com/outside/magazine/0598/9805big.html.

Duane, D. 1998b. "Something Wicked This Way Comes." *Outside Magazine,* May. http://outside.away.com/outside/magazine/0598/9805surf.html.

Duane, D. 2004. "Laird Hamilton: Big Wave Surfer." *Outside Magazine,*
    December.   http://outside.away.com/outside/features/200412/laird-
    hamilton_1.html.

"Dungeons Delivers." 2009. *Surfline,* August 18. http://www.surfline.com/
    surf-news/xxl-update-dungeons-delivers-twiggy-long-marr—sa-crew-
    score-capetowns-biggest-wave_29714/1/.

"Dry Water." 2009. *Tracks,* October: 128–29.

Esch, T., and G. Stefano. 2004. "The Neurobiology of Pleasure, Reward
    Processes, Addiction and their Health Implications." *Neuroendocri-
    nology Letters* 25 (4): 235–51.

Evers, C. 2004. "Men Who Surf." *Cultural Studies Review* 10 (1): 27–41.

Evers, C. 2006. "How to Surf." *Journal of Sport and Social Issues* 30 (3):
    229–43.

Evers, C. 2009. "Shark Island Pits and Safety Maps: The Cronulla Race
    Riot." *Kurungabaa: A Journal of Literature, History and Ideas for
    Surfers* 2 (1): 79–86.

Evers, C. 2010. *Notes for a Young Surfer.* Melbourne, Australia: Mel-
    bourne University Press.

Extreme Surfing. 2000. Prod. John Scheer, Dir. Rob Englehardt, 50 min-
    utes, Discovery Channel, DVD.

Faen, J. 2001. "Ross Clark-Jones Wins the Eddie Aikau." *The Glide,* Janu-
    ary 13.

Farmer, R. 1992. "Surfing: Motivation, Values and Culture." *Journal of
    Sport Behaviour* 15: 241–64.

Finnegan, W. 1992. "Playing Doc's Games." *New Yorker,* August 24:
    34–59.

Finney, B. 1959. "Surfing in Ancient Hawaii." *Journal of the Polynesian
    Society* 68 (5): 327–47.

Finney, B., and J. Houston. 1996. *Surfing: A History of the Ancient Hawai-
    ian Sport.* San Francisco: Pomegranate Artbooks.

Fisher, K. 2007. "Miki Dora." In *Berkshire Encyclopedia of Extreme
    Sports,* ed. D. Booth and H. Thorpe, 85–86. Great Barrington, Mass.:
    Berkshire Publishing.

Fitzjames, C. 2009. "Big Wave." *Summer Report,* Radio New Zealand
    National, January 5, 9:07.

Foo, M. 1985. "Occurrence at Waimea Bay." *Surfing,* June: 66–70 and
    88–89.

Ford, N., and D. Brown. 2006. *Surfing and Social Theory: Experience, Embodiment and Narrative of the Dream Glide.* London: Routledge.

Fordham, M. 2008. *The Book of Surfing: The Killer Guide.* London: Transworld Publishers.

Fountain, H. 2010. "Advances in Oil Spill Cleanup Lag Since Valdez." *New York Times,* June 24. http://www.nytimes.com/2010/06/25/us/25clean.html?emc=eta1.

Franken, I., C. Zijlstra, and P. Muris. 2006. "Are Nonpharmacological Induced Rewards Related to Anhedonia? A Study among Skydivers." *Progress in Neuropharmacology and Biological Psychiatry* 30: 297–300.

Gault-Williams, M. 2008. *Legendary Surfers: A Definitive History of Surfing's Culture and Heroes.* Available at: http://www.legendarysurfers.com/surf/legends/ls03_legends.html.

Goldschmidt, W. 1992. *The Human Career.* Cambridge: Blackwell.

Goode, W. 1978. *The Celebration of Heroes.* Berkeley, Calif.: University of California Press.

Grigg, R. 1998. *Big Surf, Deep Dives, and the Islands: My Life in the Ocean.* Honolulu: Editions Limited.

Griggs, M. 2003. "Bruvvas from the Gutter: The Inside Story of the Bra Boys." *Tracks,* September: 80–86.

Grissim, J. 1982. *Pure Stoke.* New York: Harper Colophon Books.

Grotzinger, J., T. Jordan, F. Press, and R. Siever. 2007. *Understanding Earth.* 5th ed. New York: W. H. Freeman.

Hamilton, L. 2002. "Interview." *TowSurfing.com,* September 25. http://www.towsurfer.com/ViewContent.asp?ContentID=814.

Hamilton, L. 2008. *Force of Nature.* New York: Rodale.

Hemmings, F. 1997. *The Soul of Surfing.* New York: Thunder's Mouth Press.

Hollinger, K. 1975. "An Alternative Viewpoint." *Surfer,* August/September: 38–40.

Horan, C. undated. "Cheyne Horan and Preparing for Big Wave Surfing," CheyneHoran.com.au. http://www.cheynehoran.com.au/redbullinterviews.html.

Hynd, D. 1989. "Felipe Pomar." *Surfer,* September: 92–95.

Irwin, J. 1973. "Surfing: The Natural History of an Urban Scene." *Urban Life and Culture* 2 (2): 131–60.

Jarratt, P. 1977a. "Jaw War on the North Shore." *Surfer,* February/March: 46–48.

Jarratt, P. 1977b. "A Profile of Graham Cassidy." *Tracks,* December: 16–17.

Jarratt, P. 1997. *Mr Sunset: The Jeff Hakman Story.* London: Gen X Publishing.

Jarratt, P. 2006. *The Mountain and the Wave: The Quiksilver Story.* Huntington Beach, Calif.: Quiksilver.

Jarratt, P. 2007. "The Puzzle of Midget." *Surfer's Journal* 16 (3): 50–69.

Jarvis, C. 2001. "J-Bay Underground." *Tracks,* March: 62–64.

Jarvis, C. 2009. "Fight Club." *Waves,* July: 86–90.

Jenkins, B. 1993. "The Next Realm." *Surfer,* December: 48–55 and 88.

Jenkins, B. 1997. "Laird Hamilton: 20th Century Man." *Australian Surfer's Journal* 1 (1): 84–121.

Jenkins, B. 1998. "Rediscovering the Old Stoke: Ken Bradshaw at 45." SFGate.Com, April 16. http://articles.sfgate.com/1998-04-16/sports/ 17717588_1_ken-bradshaw-tow-in-surfing-greg-noll.

Jenkins, B. 1999. *North Shore Chronicles: Big Wave Surfing in Hawaii.* 2nd ed. Berkeley, Calif.: Frog.

Jones, C. 2005. "Sons of Beaches." *Australian Story,* ABC Radio, November 7. http://www.abc.net.au/austory/content/2005/s1500406.htm.

Kampion, D. 1997. *Stoked: A History of Surf Culture.* Los Angeles: General Publishing.

Kampion, D. 2007. *Greg Noll: The Art of the Surfboard.* Salt Lake City: Gibbs Smith.

Kahanamoku, D., and J. Brennan. 1972. *Duke Kahanamoku's World of Surfing.* Sydney: Angus and Robertson.

Kennedy, L. 2009a. "Straight Shooter's Lament." *Tracks,* November: 10.

Kennedy, L. 2009b. "The Magnificent Seven." *Tracks,* November: 34–47.

Kinimaka, T. 2008. *Profile.* Available at: http://live.quiksilver.com/2008/ bigwave/profiles.php#titus.

Kotler, S. 2006. *West of Jesus: Surfing, Science, and the Origins of Belief.* New York: Bloomsbury.

Krantz, M. 2008. "Surfer Rides Business Wave." *USA Today,* July 18: 1B–2B.

Laird. 2001. Prod. B. Williams, L. Hamilton, and J. Kachmer, 37 minutes, Blue Field Entertainment and Laird Hamilton, DVD.

LaTourrette, D. 2005. "Nature or Nurture." *The Surfer's Path* 50: 11–19.

Lee, B. 2002. "Slater Rips to Aikau Victory." *Star Bulletin* (Honolulu), January 8. http://archives.starbulletin.com/2002/01/08/sports/story1. html.

Little, B. 1989. "Fade to Black." *Surfer,* October: 112–13 and 141–42.

Long, J., ed. 1999. *The Big Drop: Classic Big Wave Surfing Stories.* Helena, Mo.: Falcon.

London, J. 1911. *The Cruise of the Snark.* New York: Regent Press.

Lopez, G. 1995. "Quantum Leap: JATO (Jet-Assisted Takeoff)." *Surfer's Journal,* Spring: 82–103.

Lynch, B. 1991. "The Banzai Pipeline." In *The Next Wave: A Survey of World Surfing,* ed. N. Carroll, 130–31. Sydney: Angus and Robertson.

Making the Call: Big Waves of the North Pacific. 2003. Prod. Sean Collins and Fran Battaglia, Dir. Fran Battaglia, 48 minutes, Surfline, DVD.

Marcus, B. 1997. "A Good Man is Gone." *Surfer,* June: 54 and 56.

Marcus, B. 2008. *Extreme Surf.* London: Pavilion Books.

Marcus, B. 2009. "Big Man on Campus." *Australia's Surfing Life,* March: 100–104.

Martin, A. 2007. *Stealing the Wave: The Epic Struggle between Ken Bradshaw and Mark Foo.* London: Bloomsbury.

Martin, A. 2009. "Surfing, Lies and Videotape: Two Perspectives on the Role of the Media in Sport." *Sport in History* 29 (2): 243–58.

Masterton, M. 2006a. "The Dangers of Dungeons." *Red Bull Big Wave Africa.* http://www.redbullbwa.com/about.php.

Masterton, M. 2006b. "The History of Dungeons and Big Wave Africa." *Red Bull Big Wave Africa.* http://www.redbullbwa.com/about.php?c=49.

Masterton, M. 2010. "Dungeons and a Man Possessed." *Surfer's Journal,* June–July: 98–111.

McTavish, B. 2009. *Stoked.* Huskisson, New South Wales: Hyams Publishing.

Melekian, B. 2008. "Interview: Makua Rothman." *Surfer* 43 (5). http://www.surfermag.com/magazine/archivedissues/makuaintrvu/.

Melekian, B. 2010. "Last Drop." *OutsideOnline.com*. http://outsideonline. com/adventure/travel-ta-andy-irons-surfing-athletes-sidwcmdev_ 152739.html.

Mendez-Villanueva, A., and D. Bishop. 2005. "Physiological Aspects of Surfboard Riding Performance." *Sports Medicine* 35 (1): 55–70.

"Men's Events Champions." undated. *ASPworldtour.com*. http://www. aspworldtour.com.

Messer, B. 2009. "The Regulator." *Tracks,* November: 106–7.

Moniz, T. 1990. "Dropping in on Buzzy Trent." *Surfing,* November: 48–49.

Moore, M. 2010. *Sweetness and Blood: How Surfing Spread From Hawaii and California to the Rest of the World, with Some Unexpected Results.* New York: Rodale.

Morford, R., and S. Clarke. 1976. "The Agon Motif." In *Exercise and Sport Sciences Reviews,* vol. 4, ed. J. Keogh and R. S. Hutton, 163–93.

Moser, P., ed. 2008. *Pacific Passages: An Anthology of Surf Writings.* Honolulu: University of Hawaii Press.

Moses, S. 1982. "Thunder From the Sea." *Sports Illustrated,* March 8: 84–101.

Noll, G., and A. Gabbard. 1989. *Da Bull: Life over the Edge.* Berkeley, Calif.: North Atlantic Books.

Ogilvie, B. 1974. "Stimulus Addiction: The Sweet Psychic Jolt of Danger." *Psychology Today* 8 (5): 88–94.

Olsen, E., and M. Higgins. 2009. "Surfing's Dark Side on the North Shore." *New York Times,* January 22. http://video.nytimes.com/ video/2009/01/22/sports/othersports/1231545957469/surfing-s-dark-side-on-the-north-shore.html?ref=sports.

Osmond, G., and M. Phillips. 2006. "Look at That Kid Crawling." *Australian Historical Studies* 37 (127): 43–62.

Parmenter, D. 1987. "Big Time." *Surfing,* July: 90–105, 181, and 191.

Parmenter, D. 1999. "On the Shoulders of Giants." *Surfer,* August: 88–97.

Pawle, F. 2009. "The Aloha Blues." *Stab Magazine.* http://www.stabmag. com/features/the-aloha-blues/.

"Peddle and Paddle." 2006. *Surfersvillage.com,* June 10. http://www. surfersvillage.com/surfing/22186/news.htm.

Phillips, J. 2006. "Bodybashed." *Tracks,* June: 118–19.

Perrow, K. 2009. "Pipe vs Chopes." *Tracks,* July: 30.

Poirier, J. 2003. *Dancing the Wave: Audacity, Equilibrium and Other Mysteries of Surfing.* Boston: Shambhala.

Quirarte, F. 1998. "The First Mavericks Contest." *Mavsurfer.com,* November 1. http://www.mavsurfer.com/mavs_blog/?p=36.

Renneker, M., K. Star, and G. Booth. 1993. *Sick Surfers Ask the Surf Docs & Dr. Geoff.* Palo Alto, Calif.: Bull Publishing Company.

Rensin, D. 2008. *All for a Few Perfect Waves.* New York: HarperCollins.

"Ride of the Year Winner: Greg Long." 2009. *Mpora Pure Action Sports.* http://video.mpora.com/watch/Pc4HgpotU/.

Riding Giants. 2004. Prod. Agi Orsi, Stacy Peralta, and Jake Kachmer, Dir. Stacy Peralta, 97 minutes, Sony Pictures, DVD.

Rinehart, R. 2000. "Arriving Sport: Alternatives to Formal Sports." In *Handbook of Sports Studies,* ed. J. Coakley and E. Dunning, 504–19. London: Sage.

Rinehart, R. 2003. "Dropping into Sight: Commodification and Co-optation of In-line Skating." In *To the Extreme: Alternative Sports, Inside and Out,* ed. R. Rinehart and S. Sydnor, 27–51. New York: State University of New York Press.

Rosenblitt, J. C., H. Soler, S. E. Johnson, and D. M. Quadagno. 2001. "Sensation Seeking and Hormones in Men and Women: Exploring the Link." *Hormones and Behavior* 40 (3): 396–402.

Sanders, M. 2005. "Artificial Reef." *Surfline.* http://www.surfline.com/mag/features/artificial_reef/html/text.html.

Sheese, B. E., P. M. Voelker, M. K. Rothbart, and M. I. Posner. 2007. "Parenting Quality Interacts with Genetic Variation in Dopamine Receptor D4 to Influence Temperament in Early Childhood." *Development and Psychopathology* 19: 1039–46.

Shorty. 2005. "The Devil in Green." *Tracks,* October: 22–34.

Silber, I. 1970. *The Cultural Revolution: A Marxist Analysis.* New York: Times Change Press.

Slater, E. 2007. "The Joy of Paddle." *Surfing,* July: 114–123.

Slater, K. 2008. "KS9: Mind, Body, Surf Documentary." Surf.Quiksilver.com. http://surf.quiksilver.com/riders/rider_detail.aspx?riderid=169.

Smith, J. 1996. "The Apprenticeship of Jay Moriarty." *Surfer's Journal,* Spring: 104–9.

Spencer, T. 1974. "Interview." *Tracks,* August: 9–12.

Stecyk, C. R., and D. Kampion. 2005. *Dora Lives: The Authorized Story of Miki Dora.* Santa Barbara, Calif.: T. Adler.

Step into Liquid. 2003. Prod. John-Paul Beeghly, Dir. Dana Brown, 88 minutes, Rialto, DVD.

Storm Surfers. 2007. Prods. Marcus Gillezeau and Chris Nelius, Dirs. Chris Nelius and Justin McMillan, 48 minutes, Discovery Channel, DVD.

Strapped: The Origins of Tow-in Surfing. 2002. Prods. Bobby Williams and Jane Kachmer, 27 minutes, Blue Field / Strapped LLC, DVD.

"Surfer Andy Irons Dead: Police Probe Drug Overdose," 2010. *Stuff.co. nz.* November 3. http://www.stuff.co.nz/sport/other-sports/4303035/Surfer-Andy-Irons-dead-police-probe-drug-overdose.

Surfers: The Movie—Then and Now. 2008. Prod. Bill Delaney, Exec. Prod. Graham Stapelberg, 60 minutes, Billabong, DVD.

"Surf Forecasting." undated. *WaveWatch: Weather, Waves, News.*

The Endless Summer. 1966. Prod. and dir. Bruce Brown, 95 minutes, Image Entertainment, DVD.

The Endless Summer II. 1994. Prod. and dir. Bruce Brown, 105 minutes, New Line Productions, DVD.

"The Launch." 1993. HawaiianWaterPatrol.com. http://www.hawaiianwaterpatrol.com/HWP.htm.

The Mountain and the Wave. 2006. Exec. Prod. Phil Jarratt, Prod. Alan Gibby, 107 minutes, Quiksilver Entertainment, DVD.

"The Quiksilver in Memory of Eddie Aikau: History." 2008. Quiksilver. com. http://live.quiksilver.com/2008/bigwave/history.php.

Thomas, P. 2004. "Rogue 'Bomb' Detonates Latest Big-Wave Debate." *Los Angeles Times,* May 18. http://articles.latimes.com/2004/may/18/news/os-fairgame18.

Thomas, P. 2008. "Where Danger Comes in Waves." *Los Angeles Times,* December 13. http://www.latimes.com/sports/la-sp-surf13–2008 dec13,0,1410696,full.story.

Thomas, P. 2009. "San Clemente's Greg Long Wins Eddie Aikau Big-Wave Contest in Epic Waimea Surf." *Los Angeles Times,* December 8. http://latimesblogs.latimes.com/outposts/2009/12/san-clementes-greg-long-wins-actionpacked-eddioe-aikau-bigwave-surfing-contest.html.

Titchen, J. 1966. Letter to Warringah Shire Council, March 14, Warringah Shire Council, Parks and Baths, File 20A.

Tomlinson, J. 2004. *Extreme Sports: In Search of the Ultimate Thrill.* London: Carlton Books.

Tomson, S. 2008. *Bustin' Down the Door: The Surf Revolution of '75.* New York: Abrams.

Toth, C. 2003. "New State Rules Take Effect for Tow-in Surfing Enthusiasts." *Honolulu Advertiser,* July 5. http://the.honoluluadvertiser.com/article/2003/Jul/05/ln/ln22a.html.

Trebay, G. 2008. "A Line in the Sand and in the Stores." *New York Times,* May 15. http://www.nytimes.com/2008/05/15/fashion/15surfing.html?_r=1&pagewanted=all.

"Two Days at the Bay." 2010. *Surfer,* special edition to commemorate the 2009/10 Eddie Aikau memorial contest.

Van Dyke, F. 1988. *Thirty Years Riding the World's Biggest Surf.* Soquel, Calif.: Joseph Grassadonia.

Ventura, R., C. Morrone, and S. Puglisi-Allegra. 2007. "Prefrontal/Accumbal Catecholamine System Determines Motivational Salience Attribution to Both Reward- and Aversion-Related Stimuli." *Proceedings of the National Academy of Sciences* 104 (12): 5181–86.

Walker, J. R. 1974. *Recreational Surf Parameters.* James K. K. Look Laboratory Technical Report No. 30, University of Hawaii.

Walker M. 2010. "Kelly Slater Wins Tenth World Title." *Surfline.com,* November 6. http://www.surfline.com/surf-news/kelly-slater-wins-10th-world-title-takes-down-durbidge-to-win-rip-curl-pro-search_49682/.

Warshaw, M. 1987. "The Ultimate Thrill: Interview with Mark Foo." *Surfer,* February: 58–65.

Warshaw, M. 1995a. "The Final Charge: Understanding Mark Foo's Last Day." *Surfer,* May: 96–102.

Warshaw, M. 1995b. "The Man Who Loved His Work." *Surfer,* May: 106–10.

Warshaw, M. 1997. *Above the Roar: 50 Surfer Interviews.* Santa Cruz, Calif.: Waterhouse.

Warshaw, M. 2000. *Maverick's: The Story of Big-Wave Surfing.* San Francisco: Chronicle Books.

Warshaw, M. 2004. *The Encyclopedia of Surfing.* London: Viking.

Warshaw, M. 2005/06. "Making History." *Surfer's Journal* 14 (6): 88–93.

Warshaw, M. 2010. *The History of Surfing.* San Francisco: Chronicle Books.

Watson, J. 2009. "Krispy Kremes." *Tracks,* July: 92–8.

Webber, M. 2009. "Little Steps." *Tracks,* July: 44–54.

Weir, B. 2008. "Weekend Window: Surfing with Laird Hamilton." *ABCNews,* May 28. http://abcnews.go.com/video/playerIndex?id=4782993.

Weisberg, Z. 2009. "The Biggest Night in Big-Wave Surfing." *Surfermag. com online.* http://www.surfermag.com/features/onlineexclusives/ greg_long_claims_2009_billabong_xxl_ride_of_the_year/.

"What Will Surfing Look Like in 20 Years?" 2009. *Waves* 29 (9): 79–84.

Wolf, D. 2000. *Sleeping in the Shorebreak and Other Hairy Surfing Stories.* Manhattan Beach, Calif.: Waverider Publications.

Young, N. 1970. "Letter." *Tracks,* October: 7.

Young, N. 1983. *The History of Surfing.* Palm Beach, New South Wales: Palm Beach Press.

Young, N. 1998. *Nat's Nat and That's That.* Angourie, New South Wales: Nymboida Press.

Young, N. 2000. *Surf Rage: A Surfer's Guide to Turning Negatives into Positives.* Angourie, New South Wales: Nymboida Press.

Zuckerman, M. 1979. *Sensation Seeking: Beyond the Optimal Level of Arousal.* Hillsdale, N.J.: Erlbaum.

Zuckerman, M. 1994. *Behavioral Expressions and Biosocial Bases of Sensation Seeking.* Cambridge: Cambridge University Press.

Zuckerman, M., and D. M. Kuhlman. 2000. "Personality and Risk Taking: Common Biosocial Factors." *Journal of Personality* 68 (6): 999–1029.

index

About the Author

DOUGLAS BOOTH is Professor of Sport and Leisure Studies and Dean of the School of Physical Education at the University of Otago (New Zealand). His books include *The Race Game* (1998), *Australian Beach Cultures* (2001), and *The Field* (2005). He serves on the editorial boards of *Journal of Sport History* and *Sport History Review* and is an executive member of the Australian Society for Sport History.